A JOURNEY OF RICHES

LIBERATE YOUR STRUGGLES

11 Stories To Boost Your Motivation

A Journey Of Riches - Liberate your Struggles
11 stories to boost your motivation © 2019

Copyright © 2019 John Spender
This work is copyright. Apart from any use as permitted under the Copyright Act 1968, no part may be reproduced, copied, scanned, stored in a retrieval system, recorded or transmitted, in any form or by any means, without the prior permission of the publisher.

The rights of John Spender to be identified as the primary author of this work has been asserted by him under the Copyright Amendment (Moral Rights) Act 2000 Disclaimer.

The author and publishers have used their best efforts in preparing this book and disclaim liability arising directly and indirectly, consequential or otherwise from its contents.

All reasonable efforts have been made to obtain necessary copyright permissions. Any omissions or errors are unintentional and will, if brought to the attention of the publishers, be corrected in future impressions and printings.

Published by Motion Media International
Editing: Gwendolyn Parker, Chris Drabenstott and Donna Barclay
Cover Design: Motion Media International
Typesetting & Assembly: Motion Media International
Printing: Amazon and IngramSparks

Creator: John Spender - Primary Author
Title: *A Journey Of Riches - Liberate your Struggles*
ISBN Digital: 978-1-925919-08-0
ISBN Print: 978-1-925919-09-7
Subjects: Self-Help, Motivation/Inspiration and Spirituality.

Acknowledgements

Reading and writing is a gift that too few give to themselves. It is such a powerful way to reflect and gain closure from the past, reading and writing is a therapeutic process. The experience raises one's self-esteem, confidence, and awareness of self.

I learned this when I created the first book in the *A Journey Of Riches* series, which is, now one of eighteen books with over 190 different co-authors from thirty-eight different countries. It's not easy to write about your own personal experiences and I honor and respect every one of the authors who has collaborated in the series thus far.

For many of the authors, English is their second language, which is a significant achievement in itself. In curating this anthology of short stories, I have been touched by the amount of generosity, gratitude, and shared energy that this experience has given everyone.

The inspiration for *A Journey Of Riches, Liberate your Struggles* came from my own experience of struggling with my challenges, seeking my dreams and developing a fascination as to why some people succeed liberating their struggles and why some people stay the same.

Of course, I could not have created this book without the eleven other co-authors who each said YES when I asked them to share their insights and wisdom into their journey of overcoming their struggles. Just like each chapter in this book makes for inspiring reading, each story represents one chapter in the life of each of the authors, with the chief aim of having you, the reader, living a more inspired life.

I'd like to thank all the authors for entrusting me with their unique memories, encounters, and wisdom. Thank you for sharing and opening the door to your soul so that others may learn from your experience, may the readers glean confidence from your successes and wisdom from your failures.

Thank you to my family, I know you are proud of me in how far I have come from that 10-year-old boy who was learning how to read and write at a basic level. Mom, Robert, Dad, Merril, my brother Adam and his daughter Krystal, my sister Hollie, her partner Brian, my nephew Charlie and my niece, Heidi. Also my grandparents Gran and Pop who are alive and well and Ma and Pa who now rest in peace. They accept me just the way I am with all my travels and adventures around the world.

Thanks to all the team at MotionMediaInternational who have done an excellent job at editing and collating this book. It has been a pleasure working with you all on this successful project, and I thank you for your patience in dealing with the various changes and adjustments along the way.

Thank you, the reader for having the courage to look at your life and how you can improve your future in a fast and rapidly changing world.

And I'd enjoy connecting with readers, as I love sharing stories. You can email me here: jrspender7@gmail.com

Thank you again to my fellow co-authors: Brian Wood, Sonja Stamenova, Georgiana Zor, Lillian Tahuri, Jason Stein, Anastasia Gunawan, Joy Chien, Amy Suiter, Andrea Daylor, Erin Levee.

I hope you have enjoyed this co-authored experience as much as I have.

With gratitude

John Spender

Praise for *A Journey Of Riches* Book Series

"The *A Journey Of Riches* book series is a great collection of inspiring short stories that will leave you wanting more!"
~ Alex Hoffmann, Network Marketing Guru.

"If you are looking for an inspiring read to get you through any change, this is it!! This book is filled with many gripping perspectives, from a collection of successful international authors with a tonne of wisdom to share."
~ Theera Phetmalaigul, Entrepreneur/Investor.

"*A Journey Of Riches* is an empowering series that implements two simple words in overcoming life's struggles.

By diving into the meaning of the words "problem" and "challenge," you will find yourself motivated to believe in the triumph of perseverance. With many different authors from all around the world, coming together to share different stories of life's trials, you will find yourself drenched in encouragement to push through even the darkest of battles.

The stories are heartfelt personal shares of moving through and transforming challenges into rich life experiences.

The book will move, touch and inspire your spirit to face and overcome any of life's adversities. A truly inspirational read. Thank you for being the kind open soul you are John!!"
~ Casey Plouffe, Seven Figure Network Marketer.

"A must-read for anyone facing major changes or challenges in life right now. This book will give you the courage to move through any struggle with confidence, grace, and ease."
~ Jo-Anne Irwin - Transformational Coach & Best Selling Author.

"I have enjoyed the *Journey of Riches* book series. Each person's story is written from the heart and everyone's journey different. We all have a story to tell, and John Spender does an amazing job of finding authors and combining their stories, into uplifting books." ~ Liz Misner Palmer, Foreign Service Officer.

"A timely read as I'm facing a few changes right now. I liked the various insights from the different authors. This book will inspire you to move through any challenge or change that you are experiencing." ~ David Ostrand, Business Owner.

"I've known John Spender for a while now, and I was blessed with an opportunity to be in book four in the series. I know that you will enjoy this new journey like the rest of the books in the series. The collection of stories will assist you with making changes, to deal with challenges and to see that transformation is possible for your life." ~ Charlie O'shea, Entrepreneur.

"*A Journey of Riches* series will draw you in and help you dig deep into your soul. Every author has an unbelievable life story of purpose inside of them. John Spender is dedicated to bringing peace, love, and adventure to the world of his readers! Dive into this series, and you will be transformed!!"
~ Jeana Matichak, Author of *Finding Peace*.

"Awesome! Truly inspirational! It is amazing what the human spirit can achieve and overcome! Highly recommended!!"
~ Fabrice Beliard, Australian Business Coach, and Best Selling Author.

Praise for A Journey of Riches Book Series

"*A Journey of Riches* Series is a must read. It is an empowering collection of inspirational and moving stories full of courage, strength, and heart. Bringing peace and awareness to those lucky enough to read to assist and inspire them on their life journey."
~ Gemma Castiglia, Avalon Healing, Best Selling Author.

"The *A Journey of Riches* book series is an inspirational collection of books that will empower you to take on any challenge or change in life."
~ Kay Newton, Midlife Stress Buster, and Best Selling Author.

"*A Journey of Riches* book series is an inspiring collection of stories, sharing many different ideas and perspectives on how to overcome challenges, deal with change and to make empowering choices in your life. Open the book anywhere and let your mood chose where you need to read. Buy one of the books today; you'll be glad that you did!"
~ Trish Rock, Modern Day Intuitive, Bestselling Author, Speaker, Psychic & Holistic Coach.

"*A Journey of Riches* is another inspiring read. The authors are from all over the world, and each has a unique perspective to share, that will have you thinking differently about your current circumstances in life. An insightful read!"
~ Alexandria Calamel, Success Coach and Best Selling Author.

"The *A Journey of Riches* book series is a collection of real-life stories, which are truly inspiring and give you the confidence that no matter what you are dealing with in your life, that there is a light at the end of the tunnel, and a very bright one at that. Totally empowering!"
~ John Abbott, Freedom Entrepreneur.

"An amazing collection of true stories from individuals who have overcome great changes and who have transformed their lives and used their experience to uplift, inspire and support others."
~ Carol Williams, Author-Speaker-Coach.

"You can empower yourself from the power within this book, that can help awaken the sleeping giant within you. John has a purpose in life to bring inspiring people together to share their wisdom, for the benefit of all who venture deep into this book series. If you are looking for inspiration to be someone special this book can be your guide."
~ Bill Bilwani, Renown Melbourne Restaurateur.

"In the *A Journey Of Riches* series, you will catch the impulse to step up, reconsider and settle for only the very best for yourself and those around you. Penned from the heart and with an unflinching drive to make a difference for the good of all, *A Journey Of Riches* series is a must-read."
~ Steve Coleman, author of *Decisions, Decisions! How to Make the Right One Every Time.*

"If you want to be on top of your game? *A Journey of Riches* is a must read with breakthrough insights that will help you do just that!"
~ Christopher Chen, Entrepreneur.

"In *A Journey of Riches*, you will find the insight, resources, and tools you need to transform your life. By reading the authors stories, you too can be inspired to achieve your greatest accomplishments and what is truly possible for you. Reading this book activates your true potential for transforming, your life way beyond what you think is possible. Read it and learn how you too can have a magical life."
~ Elaine Mc Guinness, Bestselling Author of *Unleash Your Authentic Self!*

"If you are looking for an inspiring read look no further than the *A Journey Of Riches* book series. The books are an inspiring collection of short stories, that will encourage you to embrace life even more. I highly recommend you read one of the books today!"
~ Kara Dono, Doula, Healer and Best Selling Author.

"*A Journey of Riches* series is a must-read for anyone seeking to enrich their own lives and gain wisdom through the wonderful stories of personal empowerment & triumphs over life's challenges. I've given several copies to my family, friends, and clients to inspire and support them to step into their greatness. I highly recommend that you read these books, savoring the many aha's and tools you will discover inside."
~ Michele Cempaka, Hypnotherapist, Shaman, Transformational Coach & Reiki Master.

"If you are looking for an inspirational read, look no further than the *A Journey Of Riches* book series. The books are an inspiring and educational collection of short stories from the author's soul itself, that will encourage you to embrace life even more. I've even given them to my clients too so that they are inspired by their journeys in life, wealth, health and everything else in between. I recommend you make it a priority, to read one of the books today!"
~ Goro Gupta, Chief Education Officer, Mortgage Terminator, Property Mentor.

"The *A Journey Of Riches* book series is filled with real-life short stories of heartfelt tribulations turned into uplifting, self-transformation by the power of the human spirit to overcome adversity. The journeys captured in these books

will encourage you to embrace life in a whole new way. I highly recommend reading this inspiring anthology series."
~ Chris Drabenstott, Best Selling Author, and Editor.

"There is so much motivational power in the *A Journey of Riches* series!! Each book is a compilation of inspiring, real-life stories by several different authors, which makes the journey feel more relatable and success more attainable. If you are looking for something to move you forward, you'll find it in one (or all) of these books." ~ Cary MacArthur, Personal Empowerment Coach

"I've been fortunate to write with John Spender and now call him a friend. *A Journey of Riches* book series features real stories that have inspired me and will inspire you. John has a passion for finding amazing people from all over the world, giving the series a global perspective on relevant subject matters."
~ Mike Campbell, Fat Guy Diary, LLC

"The *A Journey of Riches* series, is the reflection of beautiful souls who have discovered the fire within. Each story takes you inside the truth of what truly matters in life. While reading these stories, my heart space expanded to understand that our most significant contribution in this lifetime is to give and receive love. May you also feel inspired as you read this book."
~ Katie Neubaum, Author of *Transformation Calling*.

"*A Journey of Riches* is an inspiring testament that love and gratitude are the secret ingredients to living a happy and fulfilling life. This series is sure to inspire and bless your life in a big way. Truly an inspirational read, written and created by real people, sharing real-life stories about the power and courage of the human spirit." ~ Jen Valadez, Emotional Intuitive, and Best Selling Author

Table of Contents

Acknowledgements iii

Praise for A Journey Of Riches book series vii

Preface xvii

Chapter One: Just a Little Bit of History Repeating
By John Spender 1

Chapter Two: Land Lies Beneath Water
By Georgiana Zor 19

Chapter Three: The Power of Healing – Finding Myself
By Brian Wood 37

Chapter Four: Integration of the Self
By Erin Levee 51

Chapter Five: The Journey of Life is all about Disguised Lessons
by Amy Suiter 67

Chapter Six: Broken Doll
By Sonja Stamenova 81

Chapter Seven: A Pennsylvania Summer Day
By Andrea Daylor 93

Chapter Eight: A Guide to Liberate Your Struggle
Through Authentic Transformation
By Anastasia Gunawan 107

Chapter Nine: Life is Change
  By Lillian Tahuri 121
Chapter Ten: Rising Above the Tide
  By Jason Stein 137
Chapter Eleven: Surfing the Waves of Struggle
  by Joy Chien 153
Author Biographies
  John Spender 169
  Georgiana Zor 171
  Brian Wood 173
  Erin Levee 175
  Amy Suiter 177
  Sonja Stamenova 179
  Andrea Daylor 180
  Anastasia Gunawan 181
  Lillian Tahuri 182
  Jason Stein 184
  Joy Chien 185
Afterword 189

PREFACE

I created this book and chose this collection of authors to share their insights, into their journey of developing courage, assisting people and raising your belief that you too can overcome your struggles to live life on your terms.

Like all of us, each author has a unique story and insight to share with you. It just might be the case, that one or more of these authors have lived through an experience that is similar to circumstances in your life right now. Their words could be just the words you need to read to help you through your challenges and motivate you to continue on your journey.

Storytelling has been the way humankind has communicated ideas and learning throughout our civilization. While we have become more sophisticated with technology and living in the modern world is more convenient, there is still much discontent and dissatisfaction with one's reality. Many people have also moved away from reading books, and they are missing out on valuable information that can help them to move forward in life, with a positive outlook.

I think it is essential to turn off the T.V., to slow down, and to read, reflect, and take the time to appreciate everything you have in life.

I like anthology books because they carry many different perspectives and insights on a singular topic. I find that sometimes when I'm reading a book that has just one author I gain an understanding of their viewpoint and writing style very quickly and the reading becomes predictable. With this book and all of the books in the *A Journey of Riches* book series, you have many different writing styles and viewpoints that will help shape your perspective towards your current set of circumstances.

Anthology books are also great because you can start from any chapter and gain a valuable insight or a nugget of wisdom without the feeling that you have missed something from the earlier chapters.

I love reading many different types of personal development books because learning and personal growth are vital to me. If you are not learning and growing, well, you're staying the same. Everything in the universe is growing, expanding, and changing. If we are not open to different ideas and different ways of thinking and being, then we can become close-minded.

The concept of this book series is to open you up to different ways of perceiving your reality, to give you hope, to encourage you, and to give you many avenues of thinking about the same subject. My wish for you is to feel empowered to make a decision that will best suit you in moving forward with your life. As Albert Einstein said, **"We cannot solve problems with the same level of thinking that created them."**

With Einstein's words in mind, let your mood pick a chapter in the book or read from the beginning to the end and allow yourself to be guided to find the answers you seek.

With gratitude,

John Spender

"**Appreciate the struggles as opportunities to wake up.**"

~ Jeff Bridges

CHAPTER ONE

Just a Little Bit of History Repeating

By John Spender

To say I was nervous would have been a major understatement, heart pounding in my chest, alert, fighting to control my emotions, and, of course, the incessant mind chatter ever present. *What if I look like a fool? How would it be if one of the girls breaks the board before I do?* And on and on it goes. You know what I mean?

We were all standing in the park waiting our turn as the facilitator went over his last-minute instructions. Just 20 minutes earlier, our group was learning the strategy to mastering and modeling excellence—specifically relating to drop breaking.

"What on earth is that?" I hear you say. Sounds like something out of a karate movie, doesn't it? Let me explain. You take a thick slab of plywood, an inch thick. You hold the board with your left hand, drop it, and break it with a forward motion with the palm of your other hand. You might be surprised to discover that a handful of the women in the group actually broke the slab of wood first go! The secret was in the strategy which created the technique that resulted in two pieces of timber lying on the ground. I broke mine on the third attempt. It was a mind f*#k. Half of the group struggled with the mental aspect of the challenge, unable to complete the task.

> **"Whatever the mind can conceive and believe, the mind can achieve."**
>
> ~ Napoleon Hill

The theory was simple; it was made up of three parts.

1) Physiology: Is your posture strong? Straight back, shoulders relaxed, and knees slightly bent.

2) Technique: The hand holding the board should be out in front of you at eye level with your elbow slightly bent. Your dominant hand (usually the right hand) is all the way back, fingers bent into your palm and your palm forward ready to strike the thick plywood first. As you drop the board with the left hand, you bring your right palm forward, hitting the timber in the center of the board in one smooth action. The trick is not to hit it too hard.

3) Mindset: Creating the belief that you can break the board is absolutely critical to your success in achieving any goal. The best way to do this is through visualizing the board already broken, split in two on the ground. Thinking from the end with feeling, this increases the chances of living in your desired reality. It's the living from the desired outcome as if it has already come to pass which helps to create a feeling of achievement; this automatically builds self-belief and confidence. In other words, fake it until you make it!

The visualization technique that we use is called a switch pattern. If you have studied Neuro-Linguistic Programming (NLP), you will have heard of this mindset weapon. You visualize in your mind's eye the board unbroken and then you quickly change the image with the board broken. You switch from the image of the unbroken board to the broken board in quick succession four to five times until you are left with the picture of the broken board. This process works like magic.

I've also done this technique when putting a regular plastic straw through a potato. Again it's 30% form and 70% visual mindset. It also helps to see a demonstration of someone else doing it first. Watching the leader of our coaching program, Craig, in that park on the Gold Coast was one such moment when you could see that it is possible. Simultaneously, it brought up fears of failure, self-doubt, and nervousness. Being in a group of like-minded peeps who all wanted to become life coaches made it much easier to keep going after the first few times of failing to break the board.

Often when struggling with an aspect of our life, especially if it is a challenge that we haven't a blueprint for, therefore unsure as what to do, self-doubt can easily set in. The benefit of seeking challenges that take you out of your comfort zone is that it forces you to step into a bigger version of yourself, expanding your potential in the process. Another often underestimated reward is an anchor of possibility every time you extend your level of what you perceive as possible. I call them mind-blowing experiences or moments of wow. When you see what just happened right before your eyes, the evidence is right in front of you, but you are still in awe of the moment.

> **"The struggle you're in today is developing the strength you need for tomorrow."**
>
> ~ Robert Tew

Tony Robbins, the famous seminar leader, has similar experiences that he takes his audiences through. He will use an NLP induction process on the audience. He also generates an atmosphere of excitement, belief, and positive anticipation. It almost feels like a rock concert. You are given an accountability partner, setting an intention of what you would like to break through in your life before you walk across glowing red-hot coals. Armed with the phrase "cold as moss," you march across the red-hot coals, ever mindful not to look down. Before you know it, you are on the other side celebrating with your buddy.

Another anchor of doing the seemingly impossible helps to build your resilience muscle, enabling you to push through when things in your life get difficult. Instead of quitting, you learn to push through and keep moving forward. Mind-blowing experiences also break the identity of struggle. Often I have heard people blame their circumstances on their heredity or their parents.

One of the most famous self-help authors and teachers, Dr. Wayne Dyer, used to have a counseling practice in New York. At his live events he would often tell stories about his practice and clients. On one particular occasion, a woman came in and told him of an incident that occurred in her childhood, and she was blaming her mother. Wayne asked her to get out of his office and go get her mother. Naturally, the woman was shocked, asking why she should get her mother. Dyer replied to the woman, "Well, if your mother is the reason why you are the way you are, go get your mother, and I'll fix her." Rarely is the problem outside of ourselves. In many cases placing blame elsewhere is an excuse not to face certain aspects of our lives that we don't like. When you find yourself blaming someone else for whatever reason, a good question to ask is, *Where am I doing the same thing in my life?* It takes some honest self-reflection, but if you sit with the question long enough, you'll soon have your answers. Recognizing that you are part of the problem actually helps you come up with a solution. A problem well stated is a problem half solved.

Releasing Anger

As long as I can remember, I have struggled to control how I express my emotions, in particular the feeling of anger, especially if situations that I am emotionally invested in don't turn out according to my expectations. I have started attending a men's circle in Ubud. The leader of the circle was explaining that the number one issue they have noticed is how men process their anger and frustrations. I'm grateful to have found this group, as it is beneficial to be in a supportive environment.

> **"A saint was asked, 'What is anger?'**
> **He gave a beautiful answer:**
> **'It is a punishment that we give ourselves for someone else's mistake."**
>
> ~ Unknown

You see, you are not the only one going through a particular challenge. In my case, it is anger management. I can honestly say that there hasn't been a year in my life when I have not struggled with how I deal with my emotions and managing my anger. At one point in my early twenties with my life spinning out of control, my anger became so bad that I was getting into night club brawls and I even chased a gang down the street, that turned out to be just a couple of guys and a garage truck doing their early morning rounds. I had issues, and everyone knew it. I was mixing in the wrong circles, and I was behaving badly. It wasn't who I wanted to be; I was headed for an early grave. (I share the full story in book nine of this series Transformation Calling) https://www.amazon.com/dp/B07BWQY9FB I was an angry young man to the extreme, I had no idea why? I later discovered that I was terrified to face the emotional, physical and sexual abuse I experienced as a child. There is no benefit in blaming others. I found that taking radical responsibly for how I choose to live my life rests squarely on my shoulders. Being accountable for my actions was the best solution for me. Visiting my uncle in prison and getting stripped searched was one of the many red flags that I had driven my life completely down the wrong road. It's never too late to choose the right path no matter how long, arduous and challenging that maybe. Slowly I started to seek help.

Let me ask you a question, can you remember the very first time you were angry? As you ponder, allow me to share with you my first memory of experiencing the emotion of anger. I was about four years of age. I had been playing with the kids up the road, the MacMahon boys: Scott, Shannon, Jamie, and Troy. Jamie and Troy were a similar age as me, so I would mostly play with them. I'm not sure how it happened, but Jamie started busting open his piggy bank, you know the large round pig that holds your change, except his was in the shape of a large office building. He wanted help to break open the other ones as well. The offer of half the contents was too good to refuse.

In no time at all, we had rows of coins stacked up, and Jamie was dividing up the coins between the three of us. Home I went with a bag of coins. My dad was away at sea with the Australian Navy. That's when my Uncle Peter would come to stay with us. Immediately my mom and Peter wanted to know where I got all the coins. I had about $10, which was a lot for any four-year-old in 1980. I remember telling an elaborate story that Jamie, Troy, and I had found a treasure chest with all these silver coins inside. It seemed believable when I was saying it.

My story fell apart when Mom called the MacMahons. It turned out that we had broken into Scott and Shannon's money boxes. I was furious when I had to return the money. It seemed unfair. After all, I had a deal with Jamie. I remember being sent to my room and, in a rage, I turned my chest of drawers onto the floor. Uncle Peter found it amusing, telling me my dad would be mad when he came home if I didn't place the chest upright. It was way too heavy. Even when he offered the incentive of a ten-dollar bill, I still couldn't summon the strength.

> **"Take on an idea, devote yourself to it, struggle on in patience, and the sun will rise for you."**
>
> ~ Swami Vivekananda

The meaning my four-year-old mind placed on that experience was people couldn't be trusted when they gave their word. The interaction with my uncle conditioned my mind to believe that anger is rewarded: if only I had been stronger, the $10 would be mine.

That was the beginning of my struggle with anger as I know it. Unconsciously I used anger to get my own way. For years now, I've been dismantling the pattern and the triggers that lead me to lose my temper. The exploration began in 2002 as I was seeking to unravel the why behind what I did. Where do these patterns of behavior come from?

The very first seminar I attended was called Insight Seminars which took you on a journey into understanding your parents, releasing resentments, and developing a relationship with your inner child. Now, having attended hundreds of seminars, having trained people to build the skills of NLP in Southeast Asia, and having coached hundreds of people from all walks of life, I realize self-discovery never ends. It's wise to note that what you focus on expands. Doing these various trainings and workshops… it stirs up the mud, making life feel unsettled. Hopefully, once the dust settles, you'll become more aware of your unconscious habits, patterns, and behaviors. I believe that self-discovery is best done in moderation, especially the deep heavy emotional work. Otherwise, the struggles can seem endless, a never-ending loop of emotional wounds, one after the other.

One of the processes we took people through in the NLP training I used to facilitate was Timeline Therapy. It's a powerful tool that aids in releasing significant emotional events from the past at an unconscious level. According to Dr. David Hawkins's scale of consciousness, the main set of heavy emotions we want to release are:

1. Anger 150

2. Sadness 75

3. Fear 100

4. Hurt 50

5. Guilt 30

6. Shame 20

7. Any other of negative emotions.

The above negative emotions are listed because they generally arise in Time Line Therapy. In his groundbreaking book *Power vs. Force*, Dr. David Hawkins developed a scale of consciousness that spans from 0 to 1000. We move up and down the scale, depending on the emotions we are experiencing or how much negative emotion we have trapped in the body. Dr. Hawkins discovered there is a critical point (when we reach 200 on his scale) where emotions that calibrate below this point make the body weak and there is an absence of truth. Emotions above 200 reprints a healthy body and represents the presence of truth. As a whole, people oscillate above and below the scale of 200, meaning it is about the overall resonance of the person that makes all the difference.

> **"Life will give you whatever experience is most helpful for the evolution of your consciousness."**
>
> ~ Eckhart Tolle

According to Dr. Hawkins, having a frequency of 500 or above is pure unconditional love, and it is in this state that we are in complete harmony with our body and our environment. The various negative emotions can get trapped in your body and the above six emotions are the most detrimental to your health. For instance, the emotional root cause of cancer is fear and resentment. This is widely documented in the books *Healing your Body* by Louise Hay, in *Anatomy of an Illness* by Norman Cousins and in C. Norman Shealy, MD, Caroline Myss's 1991 classic, *The Creation of Health*. Acting out behavioral patterns of negative emotions is what creates disease and illness in our bodies. It's vital that you release the emotional baggage that we all carry. This is truly liberating for the mind, body, spirit connection, and situations that once were problems disintegrate and disappear.

Today more than ever, there is an abundance of therapies to help release toxic emotions from one's body. I've tried and had success with the following: medicine wheel (Native American sweat lodge); crystal meditations with John of God facilitators; kinesiology; reiki; past-life regressions; Insight Seminars 1 and 2; counselling; NLP; tantric breathing; Alchemy of Breathe; Enlightened Warrior Training; Blair Singers's Train the Trainer; T. Harv Eckers's Making the Stage; MJB Seminars; Ratu Bagus's Shaking Retreat; lucid dreaming; shamanic journeying; family constellations therapy; Heart Yoga; Dynamics Therapy; Oneness Blessing; Shavasti retreats three times... These are the ones that spring to mind. As you can see from my list, I believe it's necessary to do some form of deep emotional clearing at least once a year. I also do daily meditation, weekly breathing practice, and power yoga. I can't function optimally without these practices. Even with all the work I've done on myself, I still have challenges with anger management and expressing my needs before they build up into resentments.

I vividly recall the first time I received the NLP process of Time Line Therapy. It was part of Craig Jervis's Coach the Coach year-long program. In part of the course, we were trained as NLP Practitioners and Master NLP Practitioners. The first NLP training was five days and we completed 90 hours of intense inner exploration in learning the various techniques.

I clearly remember the Timeline Therapy session being later in the evening on the third day. The trainer shared the theory and conducted a live demonstration, after which we broke up into pairs. My buddy took me on a journey to explore the emotion of anger, and I shared that experience with you earlier in the chapter. Next was sadness. We kept going until we reached the emotion of hurt. By the way, each emotion takes anywhere from 20 to 40 minutes per person to clear. One of the strict guidelines was to refrain from going into the emotion. Once you have discovered the very first time that you recall experiencing the specific emotion, you are meant to float up above the event just before the incident occurred.

> **"Since most problems are created by our imagination and thus, imagery, all we need are imagery solutions."**
>
> ~ Richard Bandler

The memory that flashed into my consciousness was when I was born. Being so intrigued, I ignored my buddy's guidance asking me to go back up above the event. Instead, I went into the event, seeing ever so clearly a baby being born. Me! I could feel all of the emotions in the room, the excitement and relief of the doctors and nurses with their encouraging smiles. The recollection in these sessions is astonishing at times. You can recall an incredible level of detail. Your five senses really come alive. I could hear the nurse stating with joy, "It's a girl!" I could feel my mother's excitement and eagerness to hold me. I could see the nurse wrapping me in a blanket and discovering that I was indeed a boy.

At that moment, with a heightened state of awareness, feeling everything at an emotional level, I could feel my mum's disappointment at her expectation not being met. I felt intense hurt, crying uncontrollably. It all happens at a rapid rate. Brought out of the hypnotic trance with a thud, the trainer was standing over me chastising and berating me. Unable to finish the exercise, I was struggling to process the emotion of hurt.

My friend at the course offered to assist with releasing the emotional charge before bed. We were also rooming together, which made it easy enough to manage at such intense training. Back at our room, my roomy helped me to release some of the charges around guilt and shame. It was fascinating to experience a regression of an ancestor while releasing the charge of a particular event for which I had a bird's eye view.

While you take someone through the timeline therapy, you ask them to recall the very first memory of the negative emotion. Once you have confirmation, you ask a clarifying question. Something like, *Was that before, after, or during birth?* As you are going through the process, you want to be a blank canvas and allow whatever is in your consciousness to come to you.

I was surprised when the words "before birth" came out of my mouth, floating up above the event before the event occurred. A crystal-clear image appeared of a middle-aged man with a beard, wearing long grey trousers and a whitish, long-sleeved shirt. He was chopping wood. It seemed like the 18th century, four or five generations back. He'd had an argument with his wife. It felt like he had said something hurtful and had lost his temper. He was talking to himself. I faintly heard him berating himself, muttering words of how stupid he was. Upset, he was chopping wood near a cottage. The undertone of his vibe was one of guilt. This genealogical experience was revealing. It highlighted that the core of our struggles over the generations has remained the same. As the famous UK 1960s and '70s singer Shirley Bassey sang, *"It's all just a little bit of history repeating."* Talk about an emotional liberation!

> **"People get really interesting when they start to rattle the bars of their cages."**
>
> ~ Alain de Botton

Looking back, knowing what I know now, I see that NLP training is a valuable experience on many levels. Often, we have points of pain trapped in our bodies and consciousness that are trigger points for emotional reactions that we struggle to control. Seemingly small incidents can mean the end of the world, and all of a sudden, the sky is falling down and we have a big drama show on our hands. To be free from the hold that our emotions can have over us, to liberate our consciousness and live a full expressive life, means to do the inner work. Releasing trapped negative emotions that lie beneath the surface like an iceberg drifting out to sea waiting to bump into any obstacle that comes its way.

Since that time in the NLP training, I learned that Scientology has a process similar to the one I went through in 2012. It was a weekend course called Dianetics, a system created by the founder, L. Ron Hubbard. I won't go into too much detail, but the process is similar to Time Line Therapy. One of the main differences is that in Dianetics they encourage you to go into the emotion, reliving it and releasing the charge. The program specializes in clearing negative emotions experienced while you were in the womb, also from past lives, known as past-life regressions.

I don't know who is right or wrong—NLP or Scientology—but from my experience, I have found them both to be effective ways of releasing heavy toxic emotions from one's mind and consciousness. Each time I have been taken through the processes, I have felt lighter and emotionally free. I have no resentment towards the NLP facilitator at all; he was doing the best he could with what he knew at the time. Holding a grudge would be like carrying a heavy load of wood in summer for no good reason or benefit to me at all. Best to let go and move on.

It was such a gift to go through the Coach the Coach training program. Before I discovered personal development, I struggled to come to terms with the emotional, physical, and sexual abuse I had experienced as a child, often suppressing my emotions and authentic feelings, partly because I didn't know how to express myself. I was too afraid and perplexed. Using recreational drugs helped me manage the pain, which was too much for me to feel and deal with on my own back then, almost 19 years ago now.

It doesn't matter who you are, we are all equal emotionally; we all experience a full spectrum of emotions—ups, downs, happiness, sadness, bad days and good days. The question is, who are you most of the time? What is your set point? Dying to our old limiting self is necessary in order to evolve into a better version of ourselves. You can do this by reaching past your struggles up for the stars, moving beyond your crippling fears.

> **"Embrace the struggle and let it make you stronger. It won't last forever."**
>
> ~ Tony Gaskins

Recently I attended a monthly event just outside of Ubud. Akasha holds monthly full moon consciousness parties. The venue is out of this world: nestled in the rice fields, this two-story epic bamboo structure, plush pool, a stage for performers, DJs and their famous cacao ceremonies. Going to the full moon parties by myself is generally a bit of a stretch. All the different energies coming together, although a beautiful thing, challenges my heightened level of sensitivity around large crowds. I force myself to go anyway. I have a good time as well, bumping into friends and making new ones.

Dealing with struggles is like developing muscles in the gym. Taking yourself out of your comfort zone and into activities and situations that are good for you grows your resilience and stretches your capacity to handle stress, increasing your ability to solve problems. Ideally, you want to do something every day that scares you, making your heart beat a little bit faster. Start small, look at all areas of your life—health, relationships, work life, etc. You'll be amazed at your progress with small daily steps into the direction of your fears. We're looking for progress over perfection. Cut yourself some slack. You deserve it.

Back to my struggle with anger. Note to self: you are not your thoughts or feelings; you are the thinker of your thoughts and the feeler of emotions. I've learned through awareness that anger is an emotion that is expressed or bottled up; it's not who I am. People don't describe me as an angry person. There is an aspect of myself that gets angry, but I'm ok in my imperfection. I've learned that I'm not going to get rid of it, but I can manage my emotional states and uncover the triggers that set it off.

Mindful practices are your best friends when you are wanting to learn about yourself by charting unexplored aspects of your personality. Daily meditation is a habit I've had for several years now. It's helpful to track your practice daily.

I personally use the app insighttimer.com. It's fantastic and offers a huge range of various styles of meditations. Mostly I use the timer and focus on my breathing. It has excellent guided mediations as well. Yoga is another unique way to keep in shape and is fantastic for laying a peaceful foundation for the rest of the day. I like to drink a minimum of 1.5 litres or 50 ounces of water a day. Again, I measure this daily by using a 1.5-liter drink bottle. As I mentioned before, I attend a men's circle that helps me to speak about my emotions. I also attend sing-alongs, kirtan, Toastmasters, and improvisational theatre, and I and do these consistently.

Above everything else, I'm looking for balance in all areas of my life. If your emotions are stable, it is much easier to achieve harmony with everything else in your life. You learn to give yourself a break, cut yourself some slack, allow yourself to be happy, letting go of your struggles. And when you get to live life on your own terms. That's freedom. As Dr.Hawkins mentions it's valuable to know what level of emotional frequency that you are vibrating, using your feelings as a gauge. Taking short exercise breaks through the day helps shift your vibration into a higher frequency. Notice how much better you feel as a measurement. Going on our emotional journey it's easy to forget that we are not alone with the various struggles that we might be going through. While the form can be different the underlying emotion is the same, our ancestors have felt the exact same emotions. May you be blessed on your journey, echoing in the words of author Caroline Naoroji; forgive a little sooner, hug a little longer, love a little stronger, and smile a little sweeter, because it is all just a little bit of history repeating.

"Stand in faith even when you're having the hardest time of your life."

~ Unknown

CHAPTER TWO

LAND LIES BENEATH WATER

By Georgiana Zor

"What now, oh Govinda, might we be on the right path? Might we get closer to enlightenment? Might we get closer to salvation? Or do we perhaps live in a circle— we, who have thought we were escaping the cycle?"

Quoth Govinda: "We have learned a lot, Siddhartha, there is still much to learn. We are not going around in circles, we are moving up, the circle is a spiral, we have already ascended many a level."

~ Hermann Hesse, *Siddartha*

I have been back and forth many times, but I do not see the struggles that tried me over time as running around in circles. I see them as organic evolution, the 'necessary evil,' and not an evil loop. As Hermann Hesse explains it in his book *Siddartha*, we can see this process that feels like a repetitive orbit as a spiral that brings us to a higher level with each experience and each lesson learned. Even though I managed to find solutions to some of my problems, I do not believe there is a universal answer, but this was MY answer.

One thing that I am certain about is that nothing is final; the status quo is perpetually changing. Thus you can always find yourself in what feels like square one, or at the other side of the coin, in charge of your life all over again. In his book *Wabi Sabi Simple*, Richard Powell says, "Nothing lasts, nothing is finished, and nothing is perfect." I believe this summarizes the beauty of life's imperfections and the delicacy of human messiness. It also tells us not to get our expectations high. So, this is what I pray of you while reading this chapter: take every word and experience I describe as it is and withdraw the beauty from its imperfection.

Each person is different; hence I am aware of the fact that what worked for me might not necessarily function for you. There is no one key to success, no main step-by-step recipe to follow which would guarantee your freedom from burdens. In life, there are no guarantees. We just have to try everything until something works. The problem-solving process of life's conundrums is based on a perpetual trial-and-error mechanism, and when we draw the winning ticket, we move on and add the knowledge to our personal problem-solving structure which we've built brick by brick, sometimes sweating blood.

Thus, my primary purpose is not to promise you the magic recipe to happiness and make all your problems disappear, but to hold your hand through hardship while you—hopefully—find my experiences relatable and inspirational. I want you to know that you are not alone in this; you are NEVER alone—you have yourself, and you have to turn yourself into your best friend. Whatever problems you might be facing, I assure you that you are not the first and definitely will not be the last person in your situation.

Keep this in mind and never think that you are not normal or that no one can understand you. If you gather your courage and speak from your heart, you will find people who can understand you, people who used to be you, or people who are you. I've heard it said, "Silence hurts more than truth." To be fair, this also works for me right now. By writing about my most difficult moments and undressing all shame and resisting the instinct to hide behind curtains, I am seeking absolution from myself; I am seeking liberation from ghosts of the past. In sharing my most intimate thoughts and struggles with you I see a valuable form of bidirectional therapy.

> **"A hero is one who heals their own wounds and then shows others how to do the same."**
>
> ~Yung Pueblo

It was around 3 a.m. I woke up feeling horrible chest pain. My limbs were numb and shaky, and I was hot and cold all at once. I could hear my teeth grinding from the shaking, but I could not control it no matter how much I tried. I thought I'd had a heart attack, so I called the ambulance. Apparently, it was just a panic attack. My first real panic attack ever. I could not believe that such aggressive physical symptoms could stem from an aching mind.

I had been finding myself in a tense situation for months. I was restless. I could not sleep. I could not think. It was like I was stuck in a torturous purgatory. I felt I couldn't bear living in my head for a second more. I knew I was going through some sort of crisis or depression, but I didn't have a clue about how to deal with it.

I had finished my master's degree a while back, and I had no idea what came next. My entire life was built on stepping stones, on pre-established thresholds designed in advance and that offered me a sense of security—a safe haven. In those moments, I felt under attack and I was missing the right antibodies. So, I procrastinated my life choices hoping that it would all fall into place sooner or later. But I had no plan, and that was causing me a great deal of anxiety. The possibilities were endless, and I felt nothing short of paralyzed.

At that time, I was still living in the Netherlands, where I had moved from Romania for my studies at the age of 19, and the only certainty I had seven years later was that I needed to start over somewhere else. But where? Do what? How? When? I was feeling completely lost, and I didn't know what I wanted and hence which direction to go. So I was standing still and at the same time thinking I wanted to go everywhere and nowhere, really. I was like Chidi Anagonye, a character from a popular Netflix show called *The Good Place*, facing the trolley problem, but in my case with an infinite number of tracks and unknown outcomes. What was my purpose? What was the purpose of it all? I hoped that I would come up with an answer before the Five People will have died.

I slowly fell into the trap of intoxication. I would numb my senses with alcohol and drugs hoping that when I would wake up to reality, I will have gotten that brilliant idea which would save me from the abyss, and all my problems will have magically vanished. I knew this phase could not go on forever, but it felt comforting to say "tomorrow" day after day. I was choosing instant gratification relentlessly: snoozing over waking up early, hiding over shining, crying over laughing, drinking over staying sober, being shy over speaking up, coffee over tea.

My confidence was low and my hopes even lower. I also got into a very unproductive relationship to diminish my loneliness, a situation which would offer me company and short-term entertainment. I knew he, or the relationship, was not right for me, but this fit in so well with my postponing of facing life and making more robust, right decisions for my life.

The pleasure was temporary, however. I should have known that if it feels too easy, it's a bait and not a real solution. When I was going to sleep, all that panic came rushing, cumbering my breath. I would imagine you could get this sort of fear if you found yourself in a boat in the middle of the sea with no land in sight. At times, I thought I was going to lose my mind over contemplating all the options which I did not know if I wanted or not. I desired everything and nothing. I sometimes even wished that somebody would tell me what to do, be it the right path or not, just to unburden myself from that maddening tension.

I was also checking social media compulsively and comparing my failures to others' shiny lives. That, of course, made me feel even more like a castaway who could not figure out life. And not being 100% financially independent was also a huge burden on my shoulders. I was crushed under the pressure of expectations–from myself, from others— because it felt that any choice I could have made would have influenced the rest of my life and that I would have never been able to undo. The clock was ticking in my head from the moment I opened my eyes in the morning until I was finally able to fall asleep.

Anyhow, I started researching my behavioral patterns and came across the term 'post-graduate depression'. I found blogs where people described going through the exact emotions I was experiencing, and I had already started feeling more hopeful that it would indeed sort me out too.

According to one article I came across in *Her Campus* (18 August 2018), the signs of post-graduation depression are: feeling disorganized, diminishing motivation, compulsive use of social media, and a feeling that you're at a standstill. Another article in the *Washington Post* (6 August 2017), also reported negative perspective of life, a general sense of hopelessness, substance abuse, and loneliness as possible symptoms. What is more, according to Sheryl Ziegler, a professional counselor and writer, post-graduation depression is underreported and understudied. Juli Fraga, therapist and author, says that this phenomenon happens "...because graduation is like motherhood: culturally seen as a seemingly joyful time, which makes it even more shameful for someone to admit that it's not."

As you could already see, I had ticked each one of these symptoms. It was time to take action. On one of the rare occasions I left home, I met a good friend of mine who sensed how lost I felt and offered me a book called *The Defining Decade: Why your Twenties Matter—and How to Make the Most of Them Now*, by Meg Jay. In her book, Dr. Jay explains that we believe that by avoiding decisions now, we keep all of our options open for later, "but not making choices is a choice all the same." The author also talks about the illusory expectations twentysomethings have for their thirties, assuming that whatever they do not accomplish in their twenties will still be possible later. According to the same author, this can damage and postpone the life we actually want for ourselves. After I read this book, I realized I needed to act, and I needed to act fast. I had to start. As Raleigh Ritchie put it in one of his songs, "...*we should try to go outside 'cause if we don't we overgrow and overdose.*"

The period of applying for jobs was most frustrating because I was doing it chaotically, with dread and desperation. I would apply to any job that I thought I had the skills for, in any part of the world I thought I would have liked to live. After the interviews and some positive answers, the panic I felt thinking of the prospect of actually accepting the job indicated that the role was not the right step in my career path. I decided to follow my intuition because I had regretted each time in the past when I hadn't.

Thinking about the future still terrified me. The verse from "Time" by Pink Floyd (the opening quote of Dr. Meg Jay's book) was on a loop in my head: *"You are young and life is long, and there is time to kill today/ And then one day you find, ten years have got behind you/ No one told you when to run, you missed the starting gun."*

I decided to change the environment and go live with my father in the UK for a short while. I sent all my things back to Romania, moved out of the apartment in the Netherlands, and broke off the unrewarding, dead-end relationship. Things did not settle right away, but I felt I was on the right path. I took better care of my health: I stopped any source of intoxication and went to yoga events in proximity to my home. I even went to a yoga session held in a nearby church. I would explore the surroundings and the cultural aspects of the city, jog in beautiful parks, meditate on the bench, and notice beautiful details on buildings and interesting cloud shapes. Once I paid attention to little details, the colors seemed to get brighter.

> **"Wherever you are, at any moment, try and find something beautiful. A face, a line out of a poem, the clouds out of a window, some graffiti, a wind farm. Beauty cleans the mind."**
>
> ~Matt Haig, Author - *Reasons to Stay Alive*

When I would feel the anxiety creeping in, I tried a stress-relieving technique I read about in Matt Haig's book on dealing with depression, *Reasons to Stay Alive*. It was simple: sitting on the floor and following my breath while holding my hand on the stomach. It would calm me down every time.

After a while, I became more optimistic about life, even if nothing had physically changed with my professional situation. I continued applying for jobs, but I still felt I was drowning in the metaphorical sea of opportunities.

Until one day.

It was the end of spring, and I came across this advertisement for a co-working retreat in Bali. The idea appealed to me immediately. The program was called "Unsettled," and it consisted of spending 30 days in Bali while working and sharing knowledge and experience with others. This retreat was aimed at people who wanted to try out the remote working lifestyle or people who were finding themselves at a crossroads and needed some time and inspiration to decide where their lives were going. I actually fit into both groups, so I applied and got accepted to be a part of the October program.

The time I spent in Bali proved to be one of the most rewarding and enlightening experiences of my life, and it came at the right moment. Bali was a haven of healthy food, yoga, beautiful nature, and beautiful people. I felt I had finally reached a mental and physical balance. I returned from Bali bursting with ideas and confidence about the future. I later quit a job that felt like a dead end, and a flourishing period began for me on both a professional and a personal level.

> **"No tree, it is said, can grow to heaven unless its roots reach down to hell."**
>
> ~ Carl Jung

It was a beautiful sunny summer or beginning of the autumn afternoon. I was sitting on a bench in the nearest park from my first workplace since I'd returned to Romania, eating lunch. My break was over, but the weather was so lovely that I mentally agreed with myself to enjoy the delicious shadow of a beautiful walnut tree for five more minutes.

Meanwhile, an old lady wearing a kerchief with rose patterns appeared and limped towards me with the use of a cane, sitting on my right at half an arm's length. The park was small, but all the other benches were free. She could have sat anywhere; for some reason, she chose to sit next to me. I can't remember how the conversation began and what she first said to me, but I recall she was talking about her life, about her son, who was a software developer in the States, and asking me questions about what I did, how many languages I spoke. It sounded like the type of small talk that you enjoy for a short while, after which you feel the need to step out of the conversation and move on with your life.

Out of nowhere, she turned towards me and looked at me with the brightest blue eyes I had ever seen. She commanded me to lay the hand I use most on the bench. After I did that, she put her hand on top of mine and closed her eyes. I felt something unusual was about to happen. She then started enumerating some health problems I had—and that I knew about—and when I tried to confirm, she told me, "I am the one talking now. Just shut up and listen."

She seemed to be in a sort of a trance, and I definitely did not wish to snap her out of it. She then told me that she could feel bad energy from my lower belly area, which was eating me, and that I should get it checked most urgently. She told me that one of my teeth was aching and pulsating at that very time, which I swear to the Universe it did—bum, bum, bum it went, every two seconds. She went on and told me many other things: to leave what is freshly dead behind me; otherwise, it was going to harm me. (I want to believe she was referring to a relationship I had ended recently.)

She also told me that if I did not marry until a certain age (I honestly forgot the number), the "old ladies are going to marry you." At that time, I had no clue what that expression meant, but I recently found out that, in the past, in Romania, if a young person died before getting married, then he or she would have been married to a living person at their funeral so that they would not go to the other side alone. How revealing traditions are about the culture of people! Anyhow, marriage was and is my last concern, so I did not put too much emphasis on that. What worried me was the bad energy she felt coming from my belly.

It turned out the old lady was right. I think she found me because I was scared there was something wrong with my body and subconsciously cried for help. That day, I booked a doctor's appointment and found out I had a cervical lesion caused by human papilloma virus (HPV) which needed to be surgically removed as soon as possible.

It is interesting how little we know or talk about this virus, even though research shows that most sexually active people are infected with it at some point in their lifetimes and that more than 70% of Americans, for example, are infected with the virus, according to an article published by *Live Science*. How come we are more afraid of contracting HIV—a virus which there is such a small probability of contracting—than HPV? I would assume it works the same way as terrorism does: the more negatively advertised, the more people are going to be afraid of it, even though it is not an imminent threat.

Opening up about this subject was definitely challenging. I was afraid of being judged and being pointed at, but the need for healing myself and helping others is bigger than me. I find it sad and concerning that, in spite of the commonness of HPV, we still do not speak openly about it, and therefore some are not even aware of the risk of contracting it. A scary fact is that it does not usually show symptoms. What is more, if your knowledge on the subject is poor, when you find out you are sick, you immediately think you are going to die, or you believe that your life is never going to be normal anymore.

When I found out, my world collapsed. The shock was like a slap on the face, even though I somehow knew something was not right in my body. When I read the doctor's results, I could not breathe, a sharp whistling sound was screaming in my ears and my stomach hurt as if somebody had punched me in the guts. I was desperate, crying myself to sleep night after night.

In Romanian, we have a saying which literally translates as "An evil never comes unaccompanied." This health problem was sadly not the only one. The stress caused by my post-grad depression, extreme working hours of physical labor I was undertaking in my spare time at a beach club in The Hague, and other energy-draining activities caused my immunity to lower considerably. I had noticed that I would catch any disease I was exposed to, be it skin conditions or the flu. My thyroid was not functioning correctly, and my glands were clogged. The news about the HPV was the last drop.

Obviously, I started visiting doctors and began treatment. I religiously took all the immunity-boosting cures I was prescribed and followed all doctor's instructions, except for avoiding stress and getting enough sleep: how can you not get insomnia and be anxious when you don't know for sure if you are going to recover when you've been told there is no real cure? The main recommendation I received was that I should just avoid stress, cigarettes, alcohol, and try to sleep early and take care of my overall health. This response would freak me out even more because I wanted a quick and certain fix. I wanted them to give me a cure that would fight the virus for me. Instead, it was ME who had to do it. MY body, and nothing else.

After a while, I started talking to some friends and acquaintances about it, and I realized how common this virus really is in society. I heard that some of them had it and got healthy again, and they described how they dealt with the sickness. It was so comforting to know I was not alone in this. If they did not die, perhaps it meant I wasn't going to die either—not as soon as I'd believed, anyway. Another major fear I had which was related to this condition was the fact that I would never be able to lead a healthy life. I was imagining that I could never be in a relationship again, that nobody was going to accept me, and that my days of fun were over at only 25. Mainly, I was scared that all these restrictions were going to impact my social life and the quality of my overall state of mind and that I would have to isolate myself from all the activities that a person my age normally undertakes.

I knew that key to my healing was finding my mental tranquility, beside the daily green smoothies and overall healthy diet aimed at boosting my immunity. I had to shoo away all those worst-case scenarios birthed by the darkest corners of my mind. I had to look at this struggle as an opportunity to make my mind and body healthy again and to find my lost balance. Therefore, I started exercising daily, be it yoga, jogging, or just some mat exercises at home.

I also added meditation into my routine. A helpful exercise I explored while meditating was to focus on a word which I felt my spirit needed at that time. For example, if I thought I needed to be stronger, I focused on STRENGTH, and at the end of a yoga meditation session, I would feel my legs were made of steel.

I discovered Kangen water (alkaline water), which totally changed my life: it cleared out some other problems caused by low immunity, such as clogged glands, recurrent pityriasis, and even venom from a sea animal bite from when I traveled to Egypt and which would not heal for months. I learned how to stimulate my lymphatic system, which is the main supporter of the immune system: by taking cold/hot showers alternatively and jumping.

I also came across a book called *The Rejuvenation Enzyme: Reverse Aging, Revitalize Cells, Restore Vigor*. In this book, Dr. Shinya Hiromi, a Japanese general surgeon who pioneered modern colonoscopy techniques, described how we can heal ourselves by "cooperating with our Ki," meaning cooperating with our organism's natural self-defense mechanism. Dr. Hiromi believes that the body will cleanse itself from the harmful residues if we help activate its natural immune system. So perhaps doctors were right all along?

From the same book, I found out about healing through visualization. I had never heard about it before, and what I found particularly intriguing was the fact that a doctor would recommend this kind of unconventional treatment. I do not know for sure if this exercise worked, but it definitely made me feel more connected with my disease, created the incentives for embracing and making peace with it, and I do believe this attitude was a significant step forward in the healing process.

When the shock was over and I learned to accept the illness, I tried to take it easy. I traveled here and there, and I explored Bucharest's hidden corners of nature and graffiti. It was also a prolific period of writing, discovering new meditation techniques, listening to music, and absorbing any kind of inspiration I could find.

While listening to one of Vishen Lakhiani's (founder of Mindvalley, a company educating in personal and spiritual development) guest talk, I learned that journaling can be beneficial when dealing with unhealthy thought patterns. According to many life coaches, journaling is a great way to put your life into perspective, discover trends and the elements that trigger those patterns; this way, you can rewire your brain if you eliminate the bits that cause you distress.

In my readings, I came across an interesting fact about the brain: it needs four different positive affirmations to annul one negative critique. On this note, one of my best friends suggested—or better said, commanded me—to think about three qualities I had every time I spoke or thought something negative about myself. Little by little, if you try it, you will notice a considerable improvement in your thought patterns.

I also forced myself to see the positives in the struggle I was going through. With regards to the illness I was suffering, I came up with a few things to express gratitude for: my supporting family, having the financial resources to treat myself, having a good doctor, getting the illness diagnosed in its early stages, Kangen water, and so many others. When you are struggling, I believe it is very important to think about things that you can be grateful for and remember them constantly.

The healing process for me was an emotional rollercoaster. To best illustrate that, I will show you some excerpts from my diary:

"I lost my appetite. I cried shortly today, it feels like everything is upside down even though it isn't. Everything seems so futile. I want the life I have now, but with the past year cut out of it. I question the meaning of it all - what do I have left? I need to become self-sufficient again and keep sickness away. But it's so damn hard... I feel so alone. I need to find out the root of all these problems and act on them. I need to become the best version of myself."

"This moment I feel grateful for everything I have. I still can't feel grateful for all I am, but I am confident I will get there. I want to learn, to grow, to inhale myself and exhale art. I want to develop my intuition and creativity. I want to wake up at 6 am every morning, to read, to get inspired, to meditate, and move. When I think about this past year, I realize how strong I actually am, and that my body wishes to survive. I want to get to love my body again-to admire it, to appreciate it, to be grateful to it, to see it beautiful and attractive. What's important is how I see myself, and I will fight to find my long-lost self-love."

"You are so much stronger now. With every hardship, you are one step closer to becoming indestructible. You are invincible. Your experiences are a part of you, and you should be proud

of them and not feel ashamed about or deny them. People go through terrible things every day. There are only two options: letting yourself get crashed by the difficulty of what you have been through, or power through it, grow and shine."

"With everything that has happened to you, you can either feel sorry for yourself or treat what has happened as a gift. Everything is either an opportunity to grow or an obstacle to keep you from growing. You get to choose."

~Wayne Dyer

I firmly believe that any negative experience can be turned into a positive one. I trust that, if you do not give up, opportunities will stem from your struggles. For me, the living proof is in the very words you are reading at this moment: if I hadn't been depressed, I would not have seen the opportunity to go to Bali. If I hadn't gone to Bali, where I met John Spender, who offered me the chance to be a part of this book, I would never have written this chapter.

Sometimes, you have to leave aside your fears and just dive in courageously trusting that land lies beneath the water. In time you will get to master the art of free diving, but what's essential is to jump and try holding your breath as much as you can handle. I believe it is crucial to talk or write about our hardships because it is the only way that we will understand the problem and thus take the first step in the process of solving it. It is a great way to get closure as well—as I am doing through writing this chapter. Sharing our stories helps people *normalize* their experiences and stop feeling that crippling fear of the unknown, because they find other people who can relate, who have been there and not only survived but were reborn from the ashes stronger than before.

I think that to evolve from our struggles we need to get some perspective, make peace with the thought that we cannot change the facts, and try to see even the most hidden silver linings. Unfortunately, we cannot turn back time, and we cannot stick broken things together the way they were. In the Japanese philosophy called wabi-sabi, a broken vase is considered even more beautiful than before it was broken, because it has a story. What we can do is change our attitude towards our struggles, accept them and work with what we have left.

Nothing lasts forever; things are continuously changing. Thank Universe for inertia! If you feel that you need salvation or you need a hero, just look in the mirror. If you feel like a victim, don't forget that your mind is your one and only savior. You can count on yourself, now and always. You are stronger than you think; you just have to point that out to yourself, day after day continually, and never stop being your most trustworthy ally, your own Govinda.

And remember: **"The wound is the place where the Light enters you."**

"Don't let how you feel make you forget what you deserve."

~ Unknown

CHAPTER THREE

❖

THE POWER OF HEALING – FINDING MYSELF

By Brian Wood

"**I knew it!**"
Maybe this was your reaction upon learning the identity of the killer in the mystery novel you've been reading. Perhaps that's what you yelled when your favorite sports team snatched defeat from the jaws of victory. My I-knew-it moment was a little different. Despite realizing there was more to life, my unconscious strategy enabled me to avoid thinking about finding myself and pursuing my passion.

Greatness exists within each of us, but our gifts are often overlooked or ignored. It's frequently easier to focus on the self-inflicted distractions as opposed to metacognition (thinking about thinking). We convince ourselves that we're too busy, but the reality is that, without thinking deeply and intentionally, we don't leverage our superpowers.

For almost 30 years, I spent most of my time chasing numbers in Corporate America. Now I'm a believer that regardless of our surroundings we all have an obligation to elevate each person we interact with. It's not just a nice thing to do; it's our responsibility. We are always surrounded by these opportunities, whether it's the brief time shared with a waiter/waitress during lunch or a quick conversation with the office cleaning crew. We're surrounded by opportunities to improve the room we enter, both in our personal and professional lives—including in the Corporate America arena.

However, a bigger stage with more significant influence is what I craved most. Not a small percentage of time was dedicated to this cause in between chasing numbers and completing a seemingly endless list of tasks. I'm talking about full-time, "all in" dedication to changing the world!

I knew it – I knew it – I knew I was created to do more than complete tasks. I knew God would hear my prayers: "Please help me become the person you designed me to be." I realized that the power of prayer is real but must also be combined with additional effort and action.

We chase the endless list of tasks. We collect a staggering number of work hours. We wear these hours like a badge of honor in an insane contest until this lifestyle becomes our identity. We are rewarded for demonstrating this ideology. I was no different and was on a path toward a life incongruent with my values. But then a funny thing happened that didn't seem so funny at the time.

Awakening

Demoted?

What do you mean—demoted? I've been breaking my face; numbers are good, and this is the reward?

Things usually happen for a reason, but we often can't recognize this perspective during the experience. Based on my state of bitterness, I couldn't understand the greatness that was about to happen.

Shortly after my new assignment with reduced responsibilities, I remember participating in a conference call. I can't recall the topic, but I do remember someone chiming in with "We've got to coach our employees" during the session. Now, anyone who's ever experienced conference calls in the corporate world can probably understand why I rolled my eyes with disgust upon hearing this declaration.

These types of vague statements seemed to surface hundreds of times during the overwhelming number of conference calls and meetings. But this one struck me differently while I was existing in a dark space. I thought to myself, "I'll show them. They want employees to be coached—I'll become a certified professional coach!" So, my quest to become a certified professional coach began.

While doing my research and examining my options, I was pleased with the thought of the entire organization profusely apologizing to me for the demotion. I was sure there would be some type of parade in my honor for achieving this level of coaching expertise. Visions of formal recognition, promotions, and acknowledgment danced in my head!

Sidebar: In a shocking development, none of that stuff happened.

Something much better took place (although a parade in my honor would have been very cool). While investing in the process of earning a professional coaching certification, with an I'll-show-them attitude, a discovery came to light. This didn't have anything to do with anyone else except yours truly. It wasn't about my boss, my company, the weather, the economy…. It was all about me!

It's never what happens to you; it's always what you do about it.

For decades, I've taken things personally. I used this approach as a method to push and drive myself while believing the illusion that it was leadership, success, and happiness. Reflecting on my journey, it's obvious that I allowed people to push my buttons.

No one can push your buttons if you don't have any buttons. Think about that for a moment and ask yourself, "Why would I give anyone the power to control me?" By allowing your buttons to be pushed, that's precisely what you're doing.

Hundreds of years ago, I was an athlete and remembered the importance of not getting too high or too low while competing. It was imperative to avoid letting the media push your buttons by focusing on their positive or negative interpretations. One day you're perceived as awesome, and the next day your shortcomings are highlighted. This lesson applies to life off the court too. Don't listen to any of the positive or negative noise. Keep pushing toward perfection. Refuse to permit outside elements to control the way you show up. Always push and drive without giving anyone the power to control your emotions. You're the one with power and greatness. Remind yourself that anyone who attempts to demotivate you is irrelevant.

Why

If no one were paying you money and no one was paying you attention, what would you do? This is a question that often helps us understand our Why. Tragically, our Why is often overlooked while we're too busy chasing someone else's version of success.

A good friend of mine told a story of how her parents tried to create a Why and a version of success for her: "You're either a doctor, a lawyer, or a disappointment."

This guidance came with great intentions. However, happiness and success are personal definitions that we must create and pursue individually. There are plenty of doctors and lawyers out there that should theoretically be happy based on what others think, but their careers are incongruent with their passions, and their Whys.

One aspect of my success definition is serving others and driving as much positive change as is humanly possible. Like many people, success for me includes making my family proud while inspiring them.

However, and despite excellent intentions, we need to be aware of the law of unintended consequences. In other words, not taking any risks can be too risky! Preaching the endless possibilities to family and emphasizing the importance of betting on yourself sounds good, but not living this advice can be perceived as hypocritical and disingenuous.

Despite what the world may tell you and regardless of how you've been programmed to believe this is a success, seek your own definition of triumph. More times than not, we're convinced by external sources to be satisfied or disappointed without intrinsically identifying what success and happiness look like to each of us.

So, after many years invested with two companies and several relocations all over the country, that little voice of doubt whispered (or yelled) to me. *You're too old to make a change, play it safe, hang in there.*

If you don't know what you want, you don't want what you have. Sometimes understanding the things we don't want helps us determine our next best move. In my case, it was clear that going through the motions and counting the time until the earliest possible retirement was precisely what I didn't want. My Corporate America life was my Anti-Why.

The Decision

Surprisingly, my decision wasn't nearly as publicized as when Lebron James announced his plan to leave the Cleveland Cavaliers to join the Miami Heat. But this was a big deal for me. I had a family. I wasn't 22 years old; I had two kids in college and lots of responsibilities. But over the years, addressing the things that went bump in the middle of the night had created an elevated level of irritation. Was it realistic to believe that those 24/7 issues would stop happening? Of course not. This is the way it would be unless I acted. Despite my resistance to taking ownership for not living in alignment with my values, it became increasingly evident that I needed to make a change. It was now or never.

When you're faced with a decision, understand that there will always be reasons to not bet on yourself if you look hard enough. You will need to overcome the unknown and have faith while believing in yourself. Ironically, betting on yourself is a sure thing.

The pain of regret exceeds the discomfort of stumbling, scraping your knee, rising, falling, and rising again. And each time you fall and get up, your strength is increased and prepares you for the next challenge.

You only live once – but if you do it right, once is enough!

Lessons Learned

Throughout my continuous journey of finding myself, healing and developing, several lessons were learned, and inspiration was delivered from many sources, including the following:

- Two mindsets work against us:

A victim mentality – Thoughts of worry, anxiety, guilt. *Poor me – there's nothing I can do about my situation.* What CAN you do? People pray for what we complain about.

An anger or fear-based mentality – Thoughts of blame, antagonism and resentment. If it's always someone else, it just might be you. People who appear angry are usually scared. So, the question becomes, What scares you? Think hard and keep an open mind. Is there anything that you did that contributed to the situation? It's okay to be down. You don't have to take a positive thinking approach with a turn-that-frown-upside-down attitude. But initiating a positive psychology game plan could move you to a more productive mindset.

"This sucks!"

"I'm so frustrated."

Process.

Acknowledge.

Give yourself permission to be upset.

Then move into the *Now what?* stage ASAP.

We all experience these destructive mindsets. You may be completely justified to have this thought process—it's perfectly okay—just not okay if you live there accepting this mindset without acting. And remember this: energy seeks like energy. If you operate in either of these two mindsets, that's what you'll attract, which creates a self-fulfilling prophecy/travesty.

- **I doubt it**

Doubt is part of the process. If there's no doubt, then you're probably not dreaming big enough. Embrace this concept while understanding that, if you've put yourself in a position to compete, you've already won. Overcoming the doubt that we all have takes courage. Getting in the game and fighting is half the battle. The people who sit in the cheap seats and criticize others are the same people without the courage to compete.

"The Man in the Arena" speech was delivered by Teddy Roosevelt to an audience in 1910 and is still applicable:

"It is not the critic who counts; not the man who points out how the strong man stumbles, or where the doer of deeds could have done them better. The credit belongs to the man who is actually in the arena, whose face is marred by dust and sweat and blood; who strives valiantly; who errs, who comes short again and again, because there is no effort without error and shortcoming; but who does actually strive to do the deeds; who knows great enthusiasms, the great devotions; who spends himself in a worthy cause; who at the best knows in the end the triumph of high achievement, and who at the worst, if he fails, at least fails while daring greatly, so that his place shall never be with those cold and timid souls who neither know victory nor defeat."

Additional thoughts connected to overcoming doubt to bet on yourself:

> **"And you ask, 'what if I fall?' Oh, but my darling, what if you fly?"**
>
> ~Erin Hanson

Steve Harvey wrote a fantastic article titled "You've Got to Jump to Be Successful." Check it out here: https://medium.com/@SteveHarvey/you-ve-got-to-jump-to-be-successful-538cb7ecf6c1

- **It's never too late**

Today is the youngest you will ever be for the rest of your life. As you reflect on the different points in your life, you might wish you could have a do-over. You might wish you would have acted differently, wish you would have created that habit or implemented that routine. Today is your do-over. The more time you spend living in regret, the less time you spend being present and moving toward today's vision and your inevitable greatness.

Let that stuff go and start making plays!

- **Face your Gremlins**

Beware of your Gremlin! The Gremlin is that irritating voice in the back of your head trying to convince you that you're not good enough: *Don't take any chances. Play it safe.*

To squash that Gremlin, ask yourself, What's the worst thing that could happen?

The very worst thing that can happen is often much better than failing to act, neglecting to live your life consistent with your vision. We regret the things we didn't do—I could have, would have, should have—as opposed to the chances we took, even if we stumbled along the way.

You were designed to do great things, but you must believe and bet on you!

• **Perspective**

We have control over our thoughts and must choose wisely. This is exceptionally important since thoughts create feelings or emotions. Feelings and emotions lead to actions or results. Thinking positive, creative ideas of gratitude generate the results that serve you. Change the way you think, and you will change your life. You create your own reality based on the thoughts that you think.

Exhibit A:

Once upon a time, there were three bricklayers.

When asked, "What are you doing?" the first bricklayer replied, "I'm laying bricks."

The second bricklayer was asked the same question. He answered, "I'm putting up a wall."

The third bricklayer, when asked the same question, responded, with pride in his voice, "I'm building a cathedral."

• **The room you're in**

If you're the smartest, most positive, most talented person in the room, you need to find another room. Get to a place where you're fighting like crazy to keep up with the greatness in that space. Make sure you support everyone without judgment and only select rooms that contain people interested in elevating your greatness.

Think about how it physically feels when you're surrounded by negative people. Now recall a time when you were among people with positive and optimistic energy. The difference can be dramatic. Most people feel physically sick in the negative room but energetic and inspired in the positive room. The first three letters of the word *optimism* indicate that we have a choice to view our world a certain way. You also have the power to select those who will be in your room. The final choice involves how you will manage negativity that sneaks into your room.

> **"Surround yourself with the dreamers, and the doers, the believers, and thinkers, but most of all, surround yourself with those who see the greatness within you, even when you don't see it yourself."**
>
> ~Edmund Lee

- **Things happen for a reason**

The more I reflect on my journey toward healing, finding myself, and my experience in Corporate America, the more gratitude I manifest. This is not a woe-is-me tale but one of realization that there is more to achieve. There's so much more out there for all of us. My experience enabled me to receive a powerful perspective and an understanding that many people—perhaps most people—have been conditioned to chase things that contradict their values. They pursue positions and titles because that's what they're supposed to do. They are under the false impression that when *this* is achieved, happiness and success will follow. There are quite a few people out there struggling. And the pain permeates into all aspects of life.

> **"A successful man is one who can lay a firm foundation with the bricks others have thrown at him."**
>
> ~David Brinkley

- **Not personal *or* professional – both!**

I cringe when recalling the message I preached to groups of employees over the years. I can hear myself saying, "You've got to leave that personal stuff at home when you come to work." Easier said than done. The reality is that what we think, the way we show up, integrates with our personal and professional lives. Imagine how much more powerful my message could have been if I had provided the team with a process for thinking differently, promoting positive affirmations and a championship mindset. Imagine how much better they could perform at work while being a better father, wife, husband, mother, son, daughter, etc. We each create a ripple effect daily. A positive ripple can change lives, families, organizations, and communities. Regardless of your definition, personal and professional success feeds off one another. The notion that you can genuinely be successful personally while suffering professionally (and vice versa) is inaccurate.

We are more afraid of success (and often sabotage ourselves) than we are of failure. The following passage by Marianne Williamson emphasizes the need to live big for us and the people who surround us:

"Our deepest fear is not that we are inadequate. Our deepest fear is that we are powerful beyond measure. It is our light, not our darkness that most frightens us. We ask ourselves, 'Who am I to be brilliant, gorgeous, talented, fabulous?' Actually, who are you not to be? You are a child of God. Your playing small does not serve the world. There is nothing enlightened about shrinking so that other people won't feel insecure around you. We are all meant to shine, as children do. We were born to make manifest the glory of God that is within us. It's not just in some of us; it's in everyone. And as we let our own light shine, we unconsciously give other people permission to do the same. As we are liberated from our own fear, our presence automatically liberates others."

So, here's the end game: there is no end game! Keep growing every single day while enjoying the journey. Taking a leap of faith has enabled me to be involved with several projects I'm passionate about, including: being featured in a movie; contributing to this book; accepting speaking engagements and executive coaching opportunities; working with organizational development projects for major corporations and municipalities; and becoming an NBA, WNBA, and FIBA Certified Player Agent.

Please don't misinterpret my message as a look-at-me testimony. I'm communicating with extreme gratitude and want to express the urgency for you to live your best life, to become your best version of You—impacting as many lives as possible. It's not someday; it's NOW. It's not operating with scarcity but expecting and believing in abundance. In the words of Sade and her song *"By My Side,"* *"You are so much better than you know."*

"Sometimes it takes the worst pain to bring about the best change."

~ Unknown

CHAPTER FOUR

Integration of the Self

By Erin Levee

What are the integrating forces in your life?
What are the disintegrating forces?

We are all born with struggles that we cannot possibly imagine, and yet somehow, we must make peace with them. We grow up with different levels of privilege and understanding and are thrown various amounts of trauma that we need to receive and to integrate. For many, it is the intensity of their mother's or father's 'pain body' as Eckhart Tolle[1] puts it, that leads to a painful childhood. For some, this is subconsciously carried through life in a way that will emerge again in adulthood, especially when parenting children of their own. For others, the pain is too great to sit dormant and the journey towards resolving suffering starts from a young age.

I was a sensitive, methodical child. I was happy to get up at dawn to practice my piano scales every morning, happily 'doing the work' necessary to be an achiever. By the time I left school, however, chronic fatigue and disillusionment with the

---

1 Tolle, E: THE POWER OF NOW, A GUIDE TO SPIRITUAL ENLIGHTENMENT; New World Library, 2010

effort I had put in at school and the results that seemed elusive led me to resist and rebel against what was expected of me.

After finishing secondary school, I went to university to study law. I left university after one year because of my thirst to experience more from life. I did not want to be defined by the certificates expected of me or the accolades that might have come my way. What did the greater world have to teach me? I was impatient and desired to know myself beyond the realms of failure and success.

Things did not initially go as I had planned after I left formal studies. Depression soon followed, along with debilitating migraines. I found myself living in London, working in a fashion retail store, at sea in a place where I had no friends. I returned to Australia with the realisation that my temperament was more suited to studying at an art school, where I could run with my ideas, direct them towards something tangible, and make sense of the ephemeral sensitivities my emotional states demanded. Challenge after challenge followed until I arrived one day on the doorstep of Tim Brown, a transcendental meditation teacher. By chance, he was related to a very close friend of mine. I felt a sense of foreboding as I walked towards his door with a white handkerchief, and an array of blue hydrangeas, ready for my initiation. Meditating with a mantra in this way is a tradition that belongs to the lineage of Maharishi Mahesh Yogi, and was my first formal contact with the blistering intensity of Mother India.[2] Tears rolled down my cheeks, as time and

---

2 In fact, my mother and father were married on 28th December 1978, in a ceremony in New Delhi, owing to my grandfather's posting as Australian Ambassador to India at the time. It is likely I was conceived there, either on or soon after my parent's honeymoon.

space collapsed into a sense of enormity that was beyond any form.

Becoming limitless.

Top to

Bottom.

Limitless is our essential self,

Not bound by our body, our name, nor our place in time.

How did I find this?

Allowing myself to be pulled into silence.

Allowing my habitual self and aversion to change to be let go of,

to return to the source of my true self.

My sister and I had once done a juice fast at Hopewood, near the Blue Mountains, west of Sydney. I felt the need to return to Hopewood to overcome the feeling of wanting things to be comfortable, but this time I decided to go on my own. My strongest memories are first of a massive migraine, as I began letting go of emotional layers of self, then of finding solace in the spearmint and sandalwood essential oils that I was drawn to in the gift shop. For three days only water passed my lips. At this time, I had no inkling that essential oils would play such an important part later in my journey.

A silent retreat.

A re-calibration.

My thoughts slowed down significantly, to a point where there was so much spaciousness I could clearly see how they were arising in my consciousness.

Taking my clothes off to dive into the river and swim naked felt so liberating, as if I was meeting a challenge I had given to my 'old' self to shed the past and begin anew. The following day, I had this experience of light-filled awareness and clarity as I had never known before. I sat, in a cross-legged posture in the hall after eating some papaya for the first time since returning to food, and my nervous system just unfurled blissfully. I felt that I was integrating pieces of my timeline I had not accessed for many years. Within three months, I was on a plane to India. I had nowhere to go or to be, except inward.

Touchdown Mumbai! As my feet touched the tarmac it hit me - I was in India for the first time in this lifetime. I felt a strange sense of returning home, as if I had been here many times before. A swelling of bliss filled my body, and my energetic heart was expanding way beyond the physical form. I felt this feeling of fate and destiny pulling me. I had no need to 'do' anything. Actions would appear, just as naturally as breathing propelled my lungs to expand and contract, without help from a 'me' who was creating the experience.

I attended a Vipassana retreat. Experiencing the anger at the core of my being, hit me like a blinding light. First, it was projected outwardly, to the experience I was having with the structure of the retreat and the teachers around me. I remember thinking that I literally wanted to kill somebody! And then, after ten days of complete and utter silence, mining the intricate depths of my psyche, and the physical discomfort of sitting cross-legged on the floor for hours at a time, with one meal a day, we were allowed to speak again at our lunchtime meal. It felt as though my shackles had been released and I could participate in a vibrational exchange. I was euphoric. I can't remember what the woman sitting next to me said, but she was an experienced meditator who had participated in numerous silent sittings. After the exchange, I remember walking outside into the sunshine and feeling this sense of weightlessness enter my body. As we went back inside to sit again, the method of following my awareness around my body internally, sending loving consciousness to each and every cell in my body, brought an arousal of bliss such that I had never experienced before. The possibility of continuing to explore this sensation and its expansion inside of me, awakened a desire to stay longer at the Vipassana centre in Igatpuri, but the administrative manager would not allow it, she made it clear it was time to stop 'freeloading' as she put it, it was time to move on. A kind participant at the centre asked me if I would like to go with her and meet her family. And so, having nowhere to go and nowhere to land, I gratefully accepted the offer.

Having the semblance of family life and normality around me was just what I needed. I couldn't understand much of the Marathi they were speaking to each other, but their loving kindness towards each other was apparent. I was treated (as in all Indian homes), as a king, for whenever a guest arrives, it is customary to entertain the guest as a God.

Here the story goes blank, though. I have literally had an empty space on this page for many days as I tried to continue writing this chapter. I was reliving what began as a tremor and led into a level of terror and self-disintegration I had never before experienced. I guess it is true that fate plays a part in these things. There are parts of our story that are written before birth, and we have agreed to before coming into form. I prayed to my grandmother and afterward realised that she told me she had been saying prayers for me, so perhaps I had felt her energetically guiding me. When I left the family I had been staying with, I went to the airport ready to fly home. But sitting in the airport, I fell into a state of bliss again that told me I still had more to experience. I knew I wasn't ready to go home to Australia. I got into the airport lift with my bags and pushed the button for the ground floor. A man got into the lift and saw me with my bags. He asked if I had somewhere to stay and I told him that I didn't. He offered to take me to his brother's guesthouse by van. Outside the airport, I found myself getting into the van marked with the words 'Sun Guest House' emblazoned on the side. So far, ok.

When I arrived at the guesthouse I checked in, and as soon as I reached my room, I lay down on the bed. I gratefully absorbed the silence and lack of external stimuli that allowed me to sink deeper into whatever was happening in my nervous system.

Then the phone rang. Its shrill sound pierced the bliss I was experiencing, so I answered it. I expected to be able to end the call quickly so that I could make that sound go away and be left alone. It was the front desk on the line telling me that 'Milak' (I will call him as I have no recollection of his name) would be coming to knock on my door to give me a healing. I replied, "No thank you. I'm fine." To my surprise, a few moments later there was a knock on my door.

As Milak entered the room, I remember feeling a conflicting set of emotions that equated to a mixture of fear and distrust, but also a feeling that if I were pleasant and clear, all would be well. He offered me healing. It consisted of removing my clothes and getting in the shower. This man was a Brahman with a 'brahman's string' across his chest, which denotes chastity. He wanted to wash away my past relationship karma, and in so doing, he would 'cleanse' himself. I have no idea how or why I went along with this, other than that I must have been in a supreme state of shock and I felt that I needed to agree and be freed of my past indiscretions. Needless to say, after he left, I felt my psyche split and a voice from deep within me, called me back into my body. At this point I felt a profound sense of violation of my agency and my freedom - a severe interruption to my own energetic capacity to set my boundaries. I had been seriously taken advantage of in my vulnerable state as a traveler, and I had no one that I could call to come to my rescue. I was livid when I returned to the front desk. I had already packed my suitcase and got immediately into a waiting taxi, without allowing my anger to be expressed, as I feared reprisal from the manager of the hotel, who must have gone along with this kind of situation before. Thankfully the taxi driver was a kind father of many children. When we arrived at the train station, I left him my suitcase of possessions, which I no longer needed or wanted. Trauma has a funny way of re-prioritising your footwear and chosen attire!

I sat down outside a McDonald's restaurant, which at least provided my subconscious with some semblance of familiarity, and I noticed, from the corner of my eye, that a bookseller just next to me had some paperback novels. I was guided to, and purchased, Eckhart Tolle's tome, *The Power of Now* and returned to my table. A young child, aged maybe five or six years old, came and sat opposite me, and I was grateful for the company. She smiled at me, and I kept on reading. When the train arrived, I was delighted to be again surrounded by the warmth of Indian hospitality as a family shared with me their chai and snacks. The journey was a long one, for which I was grateful. I didn't have to make decisions about where to go next or to whom I should speak.

I had a bunk bed on the train, as the night rolled in, and each chapter of the Tolle book sank me deeper into a blissfulness and self-awakening that meant I needed to occasionally pace up and down the train carriage to stay in an embodied state. Here I was, transforming profound trauma and abuse into the ultimate sensation of freedom and bliss. Was there nothing that could bring dissolution of the self?

Soon after returning home from India, I had the opportunity to house-sit for some fellow sannyasin's in Byron Bay. In a little bookshop one morning, a book literally dropped onto my head, and I opened it. Gangaji's Autobiography *Just Like You*[3] had landed in my lap. Opening its pages, I felt the need to devour every word, and gratefully returned to my little cottage on the hillside, with a wrap-around verandah, from which I could hear the ocean waves crashing far off in the distance. I saw myself in her image, I reconnected to my soul and felt integration in ways I could never have expected. Low and behold, I found out that Gangaji would be coming to Australia and that I might be able to meet her in person.

I volunteered to help at the meetings in Sydney. I met some lifelong friends for whom I will be forever grateful, as happens in a group of people who are seeking truth and authenticity. Being in the hall was like imbibing medicine for the self. I could feel that the silence and opening to truth so palpably. I went up on stage to speak to Gangaji and felt the burning desire to travel to Arunachala, the place of Sri Ramana's birth, in Tiruvannamalai, Southern India. And so, I accompanied Gangaji from her Satsang meeting in Sydney to a retreat in Perth, where I received a personal letter in

---

3 Moore, R and Gangaji: JUST LIKE YOU, AN AUTOBIOGRAPHY. DO Publishing, 2003

response to my own that read "Arunachala is the cave of your heart. GO there and remain forever."

Following the retreat, I knew that I would return to India and heal what the younger me had gone to seek: this time, the trip would be simpler, more comfortable and more trusting, as I had no 'where' to go to. Just to the feet of my master. Ramana Maharishi.

In the words of Papaji, a devotee of Ramana, in his book *The Truth Is*[4]

"I am with you wherever you are.

There is no escape from Love.

There is no east and west for Peace and Freedom.

No matter where you go, it is always with you.

Satsang is the reminder that you are home,

That you are the home itself,

So you can't return "back" from Satsang, it is your nature.

This experience cannot be forgotten.

That which can be forgotten is forgotten by the mind,

But the mind has no access to this experience."

I had found deep integration and liberation from my struggles. But life was still to be lived. Stories kept unfolding, but it was to be seen whether or not I would get caught in them and identify with their drama.

---

4 Poonja, H.W.L. THE TRUTH IS: Weiser Books, 2000. Page 315

The relationships in my life also had fate attached to them. I had, at one point, become engaged to a man who lived in Bihar, in Northern India. I had met his family; his mother, grandmother and many of his brothers and sisters. He applied numerous times for an Australian tourist visa, but each application was rejected. I was heartbroken when it hit me that I had to choose between seeing my own family or returning to live in India.

I had to accept that the efforts we had been taking to bring him to Sydney to live were not being supported by the universe. One day, I was walking across Hyde Park in the middle of a storm, my umbrella turning inside out in the strong wind, only to see an immigration lawyer who I shouted out the words to, "why is this so hard"? I was agonising over the injustice of the legal processes designed to keep hearts separated. The following evening, I was in my sister's home and met someone who happened to be living in the very same apartment block that I had been living before leaving for India. It felt like synchronicity, and fate intervened. We were married in a Hindu ceremony in Bali, and my vows that day were to devote myself to my marriage so that "truth may be served."

For now, I want to return to a recent time in my life when it seemed that disintegration was at play. The reality is that my family carries a strong history of mental health issues, not least having two uncles who are schizophrenic, and my destiny was to encounter postnatal depression after the birth of my babies.

Having babies is not like anyone ever tells you. For some, the experience is blissful, for some, it is not. This is not necessarily something you plan for. It is not like an order you make to the universe that you 'want fries with that'! You are given a particular set of circumstances and possibilities according to your genetic makeup, or if you want to, you can refer to this as your destiny. The baby's genetic makeup is not in your control. Neither is their entry into the world. And so, despite having spent a lot of time researching a water birth, with a diagnosis of preeclampsia and gestational diabetes, this was not in the realm of possibility. Induced, and yet still clinging to my birth plan of low intervention, I had no epidural. At the most excruciating point of intensity, I was prescribed gas to ease the pain, but later, while having stitches, we found out it had not been turned on! I had to ride out some incredible pain, it was unlike any physical pain I had ever experienced, nor would I choose to again. I experienced waves of expulsion, until it seemed the whole universe was being torn asunder. And then, she arrived.

My beautiful daughter had arrived, the child whom I will never be able to replace in my heart space. All the gratitude and sincerity of truth and love I had yet experienced was made a mockery of by her exquisite face and my heart opened as I held her for the first time. I remember her little toy giraffe that played beautiful drumming music. We would fall asleep together to that music, in a bubble of our own breath rising and falling together, the nuances of her every sound being attuned to my brain.

Within a couple of days, I was home and sitting in acute discomfort, trying to nurse a crying baby who was clearly not getting enough food. My brain was a mess of confusion trying to work out feeding and nappy changing, trying to decipher the ongoing small sounds and requests this little human was making of me. I would have happily obliged any of her needs by any means necessary, but they took their toll on my brain in its sleep deprived state.

One night, I called my husband in to hold her and I collapsed to the floor, crying. "I can't do this, I can't do this anymore, I need to sleep" the incessant torture and bittersweet emotion of wanting to give your all and your body failing you is so acute for a new mother - I'm not sure there is anything as heartbreaking as knowing you are inadequate in fulfilling your child's needs. I wanted to die. The thoughts came only because I would then be at peace, I thought. Although I realised this was not a total solution. The human brain has so many nooks and crannies, so many traumas and unresolved pieces of our memories can return when placed under stress. I needed support. And I got it - my family were amazing. Knowing I could call a mental health acute care team any time on the mobile number they gave me was the psychological support I needed. Knowing that I would not slip through the cracks; knowing that I was supported, meant the world to me.

Sometimes freedom sits in the exquisite emotional pain of knowing there is no answer other than to open yourself and surrender to where you are, at this very moment.

I took a part-time job when my daughter was three months old so that I could have a couple of days out of the house and be able to return home to my baby and smile and cuddle her. The job helped me to pay for a qualified nanny. This woman loved to grandmother me, and get the dinner prepped before I came home. I was lucky. Unfortunately, we found out that she had been drinking whiskey while she was supposed to be watching over our precious daughter, so we had to let her go.

I was quite sure if I had another child, it would have to be adopted. There was no way I could consciously put my body through torture again. However, when Frankie was 12 months old, we went away to a warmer spot for a few weeks and one day, driving through the hills I saw a sign advertising a psychic. I was intrigued, so we stopped the car and I went inside to meet her. She was incredible. So unassuming and not at all the picture you have in your mind of purple shag like rugs and crystals (though I saw a woman with goth black hair who fitted that description a few years later!). She reminded me of a little boy's soul that was very close and waiting to come in. I couldn't believe it. Within six weeks, I knew I was pregnant.

Straight away, I knew it would unfold as she had described. A beautiful, healthy boy was born. He grew half a kilo every week and I was supporting a little being in a feeding frenzy. By eight weeks of age, he was doing well, but I was beginning to fall apart. I knew what this could mean, and after resisting the chemical support the first time around, this time I needed to be present for my daughter and my newborn and still wake up every few hours to feed. So I started on antidepressants. Within the first few hours of taking the medication, I went to the park and I remember seeing colours in the trees that I hadn't noticed before. I honestly realised that I had been living in a tunnel of survival until that point. The antidepressants gave me feeling back. I could feel the endorphins being produced once more in my brain. My gut was happier, my whole being was radiating again.

I summoned the courage to take my baby boy with me on a colour and light-beamer pen retreat in Newcastle when he was just four months old. It was a blissful few days, walking up alleyways decorated with chalk drawings of rainbows and imbibing the soulful healing of time alone with my son - no meals to cook, and setting the intention here by the ocean to realign my soul and my life's purpose in a new way. I became limitless again on that retreat. I saw infinity and felt and tasted it in moments of surrender and awe at the miracle of life unfolding around me, in front of me and through me. The cells of my body were dancing again and my brain felt calm and in control. It was here that I had a life-changing conversation with one of my colour teachers who introduced me to the world of therapeutic essential oils. I came home with a sample of oil to support respiratory function, and later, I found out, this oil was supportive emotionally in healing grief. Cardamom essential oil eases frustration and anger. I kept this tiny bottle, containing a few precious drops of oil, by my bed. Sniffing the aroma became my salvation!

We are sensory beings. We need touch, taste, smell and colour around us to sense our expansion through our limited bodily experience into the wider world. I realised how the simple choice of which oil I wished to place in an aromatic diffuser each morning could help me set my intention to be totally well again. It became my dream and my focus then, to make something of this experience. Through the mentoring of my beautiful teacher Deb, I began to realise it may actually be possible to create a business built on teaching people the magic of these bottles of aromatic bliss and to gently guide others into experiencing their own empowering moments of discovery about new ways of caring for themselves and their loved ones. What a miracle. To know that there was a natural and non-toxic way to support the body physically, emotionally, spiritually and potentially financially, felt so nourishing and complete. I immersed myself in all the training I could find. Since these little bottles of magic came into our home we have indeed been on a journey as a family, moving house, letting go of a mortgage, and happily renting in an area surrounded by trees and beaches, while allowing my husband to work his own hours and be around the kids instead of stressing himself out in a corporate environment. I am forever grateful that my children have this lifestyle with both their parents around for them in a way I never was able to experience as a child.

Integration of our psyche and integration of our emotional selves comes from uncovering our pain, mining the parts of ourselves that have not been able to resolve into our limitless nature. Our true nature is limitless. Letting go of habitual ways of thinking and layers of inherited stress and ritualised ways of doing things, allows for new and freer ideas and activities to flow. We are infinitely creative beings, we can trust ourselves and allow things to unfold naturally in new and exciting ways if we are not beholden to patterned ways of thinking. Finding a body therapy, like craniosacral therapy, with its gentle release of the nervous system, and adopting certain practices like swimming or bushwalking can help the psyche to relax and unwind, just as much as the body. We can learn to feel limitless: to access our true nature.

Being free is an embodied sense of ourselves, beyond the physical confines of the body. Forms of meditation can help us to access this inherent knowledge and understanding. Finding a guide, a teacher or mentor can also help to show us in a relational way. The disintegrating forces in one's life can be resolved and transcended. May your path be blessed. May you find ease and grace in your days.

"Everyone you meet is fighting a battle that you know nothing about. Be kind Always."

~ Robin Williams

CHAPTER FIVE

THE JOURNEY OF LIFE IS ALL ABOUT DISGUISED LESSONS

by Amy Suiter

I grew up as an athlete with dreams of playing softball in college, and of course, I wanted it to be at the highest level. I was just a local kid who was told by many people that I would never make it to one of the top division one schools. I just wasn't good enough. Although I pretended not to listen to what other people were saying, I would be lying if I said their words didn't affect me. I had doubts in myself and so these negative comments played havoc with any confidence I should have had in my own abilities. Regardless of these doubts, however, I continued on the journey and did all the things I was "supposed" to do to make this dream my reality. I worked harder than anyone in school and, on the field, I played on the best teams in the state. I traveled to tournaments to be viewed by college recruiters. I took individual lessons to hone my skills and master my craft and I sent at least a hundred letters and videos to colleges all across the country. I stressed over every decision I made, hoping it was the right one. Like I said, I did everything I was "supposed" to do ... I worked hard and I lived each day constantly overwhelmed by the emotional stress of willing everything to happen TO me."

On one spring day in Washington state, I had just returned home from school and my parents told me I had received mail from my number one college. Had my dream come true? I held the very small envelope in my hand. It was the size of a small thank you letter. I was hesitant to open it, but at the same time, I was more excited than I had ever been in my life. Slowly I opened the white envelope. Just as the size of the envelope indicated, it contained a small card with the logo of my top school in beautiful color on the front. Inside the card read:

Amy,

We have heard such amazing things about you, and after watching you play, we would love to invite you to be a recruited walk-on in our program next fall. If you can come to watch a game next weekend, we would love for you to stay after the game and talk with our coaching staff.

Sincerely,

Coach

The following weekend my family and I went to the game, and as promised after the game was over, we were escorted down to the locker room to meet the coaching staff in person. As I walked from the stands down toward the field my heart was racing, my palms were sweating, I was so nervous. Was this really happening? Was I genuinely getting an opportunity to play here on this field? The assistant coach held the door open as I stepped foot into my childhood fantasy. The locker room was very impressive with beautiful purple carpets and an impressive, fully fitted out kitchen. But even more impressive than the actual room I was standing in, was the knowledge that I was in the presence of amazing athletes from all over the country, brought together on this team, with the mission of winning a National Championship. They were all sitting in front of their lockers on stools. It was almost too good to be true! We walked across the locker room to a small meeting room where they closed the door behind us. At that moment, I was more nervous than I had ever been in my life. I was sitting across the table from a woman whom I sincerely admired and considered to be one of the best coaches of all time. But, at the same time, I thought she looked very scary! I was shaking on the inside while trying my best to convey the body language of a confident high school senior ready to be a part of this program. I can't tell you anything that was even discussed in that meeting but what I can tell you is I knew this was it, the place I was supposed to play.

The following four years would be the best, the worst and the most challenging years of my life to that point. I was challenged by this coach and this program and pushed outside of my comfort zone on a daily basis. I did not come into this program slated as a starter or even someone who would see the field, I had to work, and I had to become better every day.

I did exactly this and by the beginning of my sophomore year, I was starting in a position that I had never played before. During my junior year, I suffered a season-ending injury only a couple weeks into the season and was forced to red-shirt[1]. The following season I was named team captain

---

[1] I was forced to redshirt withdraw from competition for the year which would allow me one year of eligibility back at the end of my playing career.

and given even more responsibility. Like I said before, it was the best, the worst, and the most challenging part of my life up to that point. And then the phone call came.

It was December of my fifth year, my true senior season, since one year ended up being a red-shirt year. We had finished up finals and winter break had just begun. I was at a shopping center late in the evening with my parents when my cell phone rang. I quickly answered to hear my Head Coach's voice shaking with confusion, fear and a sense of urgency. She promptly told me that she didn't know exactly where this all came from, but she had been asked to leave the University and wouldn't be coaching us in my senior year. She asked me, as captain of the team, to contact all my team members, including our incoming recruits for the following year. She wanted them to learn this devastating news from me and not hear about it through the media. I was confused and fearful. I had no idea how this could have happened.

The following two months were an emotional rollercoaster for all of us involved: coaches, players, parents, incoming recruits, alumni, fans, and everyone in this program. The University that I had grown up respecting and believing to be one of the best in the country was making assumptions about the sincerest coach, and person, I had ever known. How could anyone possibly believe that she was involved with things that I knew she was absolutely not a part of! But it was not just me, everyone involved in this program knew this for a fact and so we decided that if we all fought for what was right, there was no way she could be fired for something that was far from the truth. All the players quickly decided to quit, the alumni agreed to write letters to the administration, and the softball community backed our beloved coach. And then, as quickly as this all played out, the tides turned.

Current players realized that if they did quit and nothing happened, they would lose their scholarships and would no longer be able to pay for college. Assistant coaches realized if they left, there would be no one to coach the players, and they would be out of a job, unable to support their families. Furthermore, the alumni realized that if they wrote letters to the administration and our head coach was fired in any event, they wouldn't be able to apply for her job to keep the traditions of the program alive. Reality had reared its face and choices had to be made.

Come the first week of January when we were supposed to report back for school, all my teammates had made the decision to continue playing so as not to lose their scholarships. The assistant coaches had made the decision to continue coaching in interim roles, the alumni decided not to send letters to the administration and instead apply for the coaching job to keep tradition alive. Now I had to make my decision.

I was raised on the saying "you are only as good as your word" and honesty and loyalty were deep in my roots. I knew better than to let my Head Coach take the fall for something she wasn't involved in. I knew the right thing to do was to stand up for the truth. I knew I couldn't continue to play for a University, for coaches, and with players that were "pretending" things just happened and we didn't have a choice. At the end of the day, we always have a choice – we should and must follow our intuition and do what we feel is right. This much I knew!

What I also knew was that I had worked my whole childhood to be where I was at this moment in time, I knew the sacrifices I had made to earn the uniform that I proudly wore. I knew how hard I had to work all these years to compete for this University and to be a part of this team. I knew I would lose my scholarship and have to pay for my last year of college. I knew I wouldn't be able to play in my senior game, which is one of the most special days of our careers as athletes. I knew I would lose friendships from some, or even most, teammates, alumni, and coaches. I would be judged by so many, including myself, and labelled a quitter. I would lose my identity as a collegiate athlete.

To be completely honest, I knew what decision I needed to make, and for once in my life, I couldn't explain to you why I knew. I just knew. I knew I had to do what was right for me. I couldn't be a part of something that I didn't believe in, that I didn't trust, and that was so far from the truth. So, I decided to quit in the last and final months of my collegiate softball career. I followed my intuition!

For my entire life, I had looked through the lens of "life keeps happening to me." Everything good and everything bad happened to me. I would live for the emotional highs of the good and play victim when things turned bad. My life was an emotional rollercoaster, I was always waiting to see what the next twist or turn would be. I would downplay any amazing moments so as not to be hurt too badly when the inevitable challenging moments arrived. I would be in the middle of a beautiful moment literally telling myself, "don't get too excited because when this happens, you might soon get hurt." I was constantly working towards, and hoping, for the best-case scenario yet at the same time preparing for, and expecting, the worst.

You can work your entire childhood to get good grades, be a leader in school, work hard on the softball field, and sacrifice many social activities all to land your opportunity to play softball at your dream college only to have everything ripped away from you in your senior year.

Looking back on these four and a half years of my life, my college years, I never stopped to really evaluate or pay attention to all the life lessons that had continued to happen on my journey. The lens I had on life at that time was "life is happening to me." With every obstacle that appeared, or struggle that presented itself to me, I would say to myself "why me, why again, I am working so hard, don't I deserve a break?"

I continued to see these same obstacles and struggles showing up in my life; it almost seemed as if my life was on a repeat loop. After leaving college, my next big adventure was a collegiate coaching job in Texas as an assistant softball coach. I coached there for four years and guess what, in my fourth year, life repeated itself. The head coach left the program in the fall, and I was given the interim head coach responsibility. Throughout that entire season, I continued to think exactly in the same way I had thought all my life. In other words, I hoped for the best … …to get the job, but then again expecting the worst that I wouldn't get the job! I spent so much time and energy thinking about what would it be like if I didn't get the job. Not to mention my husband was my assistant coach, meaning if I didn't get the job, neither would he. To add even more stress to our situation, we had just found out we were pregnant with our first child. You can imagine the thoughts that poured through my head all day, every day. "If we don't get this job, how will we support our new little one?" "What will my family think?" "Will I have to move yet again to another state to find a job?" "Who will hire a softball coach that is having a baby right before the season starts?" "I should have stayed home in the first place, why on earth did we even take this job in Texas?" My thoughts and emotions were all focused on what I didn't want to happen. I am sure you can guess what happened next.

It was a Monday morning, my husband, and I had just returned home after recruiting all weekend at a Junior College National Tournament. I received a call from the athletic director's secretary asking me to go and talk to him. I walked into his office and with no hesitation, he told me they had decided to hire the baseball coach's son who had been coaching at another school in town. There it was. My life indeed on repeat!

My husband and I moved back home to Washington shortly after this news. I applied for a coaching job just a thirty-minute drive from where we were living and it turned out to be the perfect place for me! I coached for eight seasons, having my second baby in the middle of this stint and in my seventh season, I became pregnant with my third child.

My passion for coaching derived from the privilege I felt in being able to nurture young women in the 18 to 22 age range and to really help them find who they were, support them through their life lessons, and do my best to be a positive influence in their lives. I really believed from the connections, relationships, and experiences I had with the majority of my players over the years that I was doing just this and, for the most part, my players really loved me.

You often hear horror stories around coaching in collegiate athletics. A common perception is that "entitled kids" are running the show and getting coaches fired over ridiculous things. I always told myself this would never happen to me.

My kids all respected me and would never go down this road, but sadly I was wrong. Indeed, my life was repeating yet again!

We had just returned to the University after competing in a Regional Championship that in my opinion went really well. Yes, we lost, but we had a fantastic weekend. I was called for a meeting in the Athletic Director's office[2]. As I walked in, I noticed a woman who was, at that time, unknown to me. She turned out to be the Head of Human Resources. They both told me that I was being put on leave as they had to conduct an investigation, I was completely caught off guard! I had no idea what the investigation was about, in fact before walking into the office, I didn't even have an inkling that anything was wrong. They informed me that I needed to turn in my keys and to ensure that I had no contact with any current players, recruits, staff or other coaches. I was hurt, devastated, confused, scared, angry. I had every negative emotion possible, not to mention I was seven months pregnant.

This was one of the longest, most confusing episodes of my life. Apparently, I had some disgruntled players who really wanted me to be fired and they had enough other players on their side to initiate an investigation. During this period, when the investigation was proceeding, I had way too much time to think. Thoughts like, "why am I even coaching if I'm not the influence these kids want in their lives"? And, "I

---

2 I was called for a meeting in the Athletic Director's office which normally would not concern me at all how ever this time was different. I asked him if it could wait an hour as I had a team meeting scheduled and I would come over right after we finished. He quickly told me I needed to cancel the team meeting and come straight to his office. My stomach dropped and I walked over to his office full of anxiety.

give so much of my time to these kids, even to the point of taking away time from my own kids, and yet they just turn their backs on me." "I obviously am not teaching them life lessons if they didn't even approach me and let me know that something was wrong before going to administration." "Maybe this is a sign, maybe I'm not supposed to be coaching anymore." "Maybe I need to be investing all this time into my own kids and husband." "If I leave coaching, how will we support our family?" "My family's insurance is provided from my employment at this University, how will we survive if I'm not working?" The talk in my head never quit!

In August, I was asked to come back to work and that is when I really had a decision to make[3]. Do I go back to coach these kids who had turned their backs on me? To this day I have no idea why they did this. Do I go back to coach because I have a freshman class coming in who were never a part of any of this and they need me? Do I go back because I need to help them learn and grow from whatever happened last year? Do I take this as an opportunity to walk away from coaching and spend more time with my own family? I was about to have my third kiddo!

I decided I had put way too much work into this University, the program and these kids just to walk away when the going got tough. I went back to coach them the following fall and promised myself that I would hold no grudges, be the bigger person, and give these young athletes what they needed to grow that year.

---

3 I was asked to come back to coach after the investigation was completed and my name had been cleared, and that is when I really had a decision to make. So many emotions, yes my name had been cleared, which should have felt like a relief, but I was also still very hurt, angry, and confused... so many questions.

I was now 36 years old, married to a beautiful human being and the proud mother of three amazing children. I had overcome so many struggles and emotions, and I was finally waking up. I had been on this perfect path all along, **life was not happening to me, it was indeed happening for me**! Every obstacle and every struggle, was a lesson I needed to learn to become the person I was put on this earth to become. The lessons I failed to learn the first couple times continued to repeat themselves until I got from them what I needed.

Awareness, consciousness, waking up and taking the reins of your thoughts is the key to liberating your struggles. We, as human beings, are running on subconscious scripts (or programs) of how our lives have always been. We start programming these scripts the moment we are born, and therefore our parents and environment when we are growing up have a large part to play in determining what is included in these scripts. Our subconscious mind works perfectly to keep us safe and comfortable as we continue to do the things we've always done, think the way we've always thought, feel the way we've always felt, and be the people we've always been, by continually running these programs.

I said my life felt as if it was on repeat and, guess what, it absolutely was and is until I made a conscious decision to change my thoughts and bring into my life everything I have ever desired! I spent my entire childhood, my 20's, and most of my 30's with the same thoughts: work really hard, go get what you want, and don't get too excited or attached because when it's taken away, it hurts! This "story" was the exact program my subconscious has been running on for over thirty years. I am overly grateful that I am able now to look back on my life and to see that every obstacle that I encountered was indeed a gift on my path to bring me right here where I am while writing this chapter.

The lesson I have learned, and am currently living by, as I head into my 40's is that thoughts create things, and I can choose those thoughts consciously to determine what I bring into my life in the coming years. In selecting these thoughts, I can continue to let my mind work perfectly by giving it new programs to run on. I now know that every struggle I encounter is part of my path and I will let go and embrace each one of them with 100 per cent faith that my desires will show up exactly when they are supposed to when I am ready for them. *Life is not happening to you.* It never was. *Life is always happening for you*!

"Surrender what is, let go of what was, and have faith in what will be."

~ Sonia Ricotti

CHAPTER SIX

Broken Doll

By Sonja Stamenova

Standing right there on the balcony of my unit, which my husband and I had mortgaged together, I was looking at the children in front of the building playing their games. I was trying to look at this as a place to be called home, the only place where I was supposed to feel warm, loved, and free. Was I feeling like that? Hell no! Every day was a struggle to survive. Life wasn't easy.

We were struggling with finances, and it was a real challenge to keep a roof over our heads. It was also a real challenge to pay a monthly rate at the bank, put food on the table, and buy some clothing for my two-year-old girl and me since most of my husband's earnings went to his gambling addiction and alcohol.

Anyway, here I was keeping an eye from the balcony on my two-year-old golden-haired girl.

It was one of the rare moments that her father took her in front of the building to get some fresh air and play with the children from the neighborhood so I could finish some of my washing.

And there she was, my lovely princess holding her doll looking at the other children's game and trying to fit in. Her blue eyes were staring at them, calling them to invite her to join the game, holding tight to her doll as if to her only friend, waiting for them to notice that she had just brushed her hair.

Only half an hour earlier, they'd both had a bath, put on matching-colored dresses, brushed their hair, and gone outside with the hope that they might get noticed, which wasn't happening right at the moment.

I was going to call her name and tell her to wait a minute until mummy gets downstairs to play with them. Then one of the children took her doll out of her hands and passed it to another. Then another kid took her favorite toy, saying how ugly the doll was, and threw it to the ground so hard that the doll broke into pieces. My little one started crying, and her father was laughing with the other children saying it was ugly anyway.

At that moment, I felt a single tear running down my cheek. I was feeling the pain in my chest, remembering the times my sister and I had played together, sleeping in the same bed, sharing the same toys, same wardrobe, songs, stories, friends…and here everyone was laughing at my daughter's tears. No one was there to hug her or to fight the naughty children with her.

All I could do was to give her a big hug and promise to get her a new doll. That was the night I decided that the best thing I could do for her would be to give her a sibling so she would not be lonely. She would have somebody to play with, somebody to argue with, and somebody to share her fears with.

Two months later, I found myself expecting my second child, and this time there was no excitement of carrying another human being in my stomach. There was no happiness in my eyes, as the last cent of our money that we'd kept for the rainy days was all gone. I was quietly sitting on my couch, trying to hide the tears from my precious beauty and trying to explain to her that there is another human's heart inside of mummy's tummy—a new doll she could play with. My phone rang, and I finally got some good news from overseas. My sister was getting married to the man of her dreams and there was to be a wedding in two months' time.

Since I did not have a wedding, I made the decision to go for the wedding regardless of the 22-hour flight and was feeling all excited to see my whole family after three years apart. That November 2000, I boarded the plane for a 22-hour flight from Sydney to Skopje not even thinking of my condition as a pregnant woman.

My heart was full of happiness, so anxious to take my sweetheart to meet her grandma, grandpa, aunt, and the rest of the family, so proud to see her in a white dress as a flower girl at the wedding, and it did not cross my mind to worry about my health and the health of my unborn child.

This was my six weeks and I was flying to enjoy them without my husband. Somehow, he'd found the money for the tickets and let me travel by myself; he knew that I would have to come back to him since I had a child and another one on the way.

My daughter was very unsettled during the whole flight, crying for her milk, and there was no milk on the plane. I had to carry her in my arms during the entire flight and could feel the looks from the other passengers, and I could read from their eyes: "For God's sake, please calm that child. We are all tired!"

And in that moment, I felt so sick and fainted. It is still not clear to me how I ended up in Skopje within a couple of hours, faking happiness and smiling to all members of my family as if I were the happiest person in this world.

We all sometimes fake happiness to protect our loved ones from our pains and sorrows. We all hide our pains and tears to protect the ones that we love from the demons that are haunting us. There I was faking a good life overseas so that my family could not see my disappointment in married life.

Six weeks of happiness went very fast. I enjoyed the wedding. Even the cheap dress bought from the markets for that occasion fit perfectly and was hiding my pregnant tummy. It was like we'd made a deal to shine this few weeks and leave all the fat and ugliness that comes with the pregnancy for when I arrived back to the man I had married.

And there I was so soon flying back to my reality, and this time what was waiting for me was empty beer bottles all over the place, some hidden in the corners of the kitchen cabinets. I still do not understand why empty bottles needed to be hidden instead of thrown away in the garbage container outside.

The bank account was left on zero and we had to rely on government benefits for the groceries. Our first shopping in two months ended up horrible. There are no words to describe the feeling of worthlessness a pregnant woman experiences when pushing the shopping trolley with groceries and a two-and-a-half-year-old inside, when she is exhausted from the overseas trip and then faints again at the fruit shop. I had some lemonade and continued pushing the shopping trolley with the men walking slowly next to me.

Who was he? What did we have in common? A mortgage? This lovely girl with stunning blue eyes? Why was he treating me like this? I was carrying his second child…and, yes, why did I fall pregnant again? I did not need this child! I hated it! I hated its father. And then, without realizing it, I started hitting my stomach, doing plenty of heavy lifting, trying to force a miscarriage.

How could we get through these struggles? Life did not offer any good with this man. We did not deserve to suffer anymore. The unborn baby did not need to enter this ugly world.

If you are given the gift of a new life, take it and say, 'Thank you God."

Life has some unexplainable ways to punish us for being ungrateful and not taking the gifts of life that God has given to us rational human beings. This is what I've learned the hard way. If God is giving you life, do not fight it. Take it and walk through life with it. He'll make sure you are safe, but do not fight it. Pray.

And there it was: 57 cm long, with the weight of 3.990 kg, the little creature that came to this world with little help from the doctors—another beautiful girl with long, dark hair. And she had plenty of hair! At that moment it was completely clear what was causing the uncomfortable stomach acids during my pregnancy.

Since I had not gotten a chance to breastfeed my first daughter, nothing could turn me off that idea this time. So, in the presence of the nurse at the hospital holding her next to my breast, I felt her trying to feed herself. My new angel was trying to get some milk out of my breast sucking so hard that I felt extreme pain on the lower part of my stomach—very sharp pain—but I smiled thinking, "So this is why breastfeeding is good to lose your belly fat." And, right at that moment, she started suffocating. Her eyes rolled, and her skin turned red.

"What have you done? Do you want to kill your baby? I am not giving it to you to breastfeed anymore!" The nurse was screaming at me in panic while my baby was vomiting. A cold feeling surrounded my heart.

"I do not know what it was, but this is not good," I thought to myself.

We put the baby on the formula, and everything settled down. She was feeding but lost some weight the second day. By the third day, everything seemed to be okay, so we were discharged from the hospital within the normal range of five days. She was such a lovely little creature, sleeping most of the time. Little sister was so happy.

And then after a week it all started. She was vomiting without any reason. We were going to doctors, changing the formula, going back to doctors… sleepless nights running from one doctor to another. I could not stop feeling that something was not right, but the doctor said to change the formula, sterilize the bottles, and wait for a few days.

This cycle would not stop, not until one nurse approached me with the words, "Do not listen to anybody but your heart! You are the mum and mums always know what to do." And this mum took the baby to the local hospital where she would not eat until the baby was able to feed, and for a week nobody could tell what was wrong.

On one occasion, hopelessly surrounded with pain and looking to the doctors for the only help I could find, I approached one of the pediatricians at the hospital for an explanation of what kind of sickness it could be. I was praying to him to help us, and his words were, "I am so sorry. I cannot tell you exactly until further tests are done at the Children's Hospital at Westmead. Your baby is not a doll I can fix and give back to you and job done."

Those words felt like a knife going through my heart. I had to wake up. No more starving myself. My doll was broken, and I had to find a professional to fix it. I could not leave it as I had a few months ago, broken in my child's arms. I had to remain strong with a clear mind; I needed to think positively.

And that very same evening, we were transferred to the Children's Hospital at Westmead. The diagnosis was made within 24 hours. There it was, my little dolly at the operation theatre with no one but me by her side. Her sister was looked after by some friends that I knew, and the father was seen gambling 30km away.

Pyloric Stenosis

Pyloric stenosis is a narrowing of the pylorus. When a baby has pyloric stenosis, this narrowing of the pyloric channel prevents food from emptying out of the stomach.

Normally, a muscular valve (pylorus) between the stomach and small intestine holds food in the stomach until it is ready for the next stage in the digestive process. In pyloric stenosis, the pylorus muscles thicken and becomes abnormally large, blocking food from reaching the small intestine. Pyloric stenosis can lead to forceful vomiting, dehydration, and weight loss. Babies with pyloric stenosis may seem to be hungry all the time. In my daughter's case, to do the diagnosis was very hard because it is a sickness that runs in the families and it is usually the first male born that gets it. But here it happened to my girl, and she was my second born.

One day I heard one of the specialists talking and explaining to his younger colleague that it could have happened because of some chemical that mother was exposed to during pregnancy, and a sense of guilt took over me. At the time, I was a clean freak and would use any chemical to keep the house and clothing clean.

During my stay in the hospital, I'd seen a lot of suffering, but I also got a chance to see how the suffering brings the families closer together. I cannot remember what the baby next to mine was suffering from, but I still remember that the mum said they were in and out of the hospital for nine months. Every morning she would get up and do her hair and makeup and her husband was there; he did not miss a day to come and give them a kiss on his way to work for the duration of those nine months.

I'll never forget the day doctors told me that the next morning my baby will be at their hands at the operation theatre. On that very evening, I was sitting by myself at the tearoom and the couple at the table next to mine was hugging and comforting each other. I was 27 years of age at that time and I would not have guessed either of them to be more than 22. One young father would drive for four hours from his home in the countryside to visit his family, and he did that every second day. Four hours each direction just to give comfort to his wife and kiss their little angel's forehead. Can you imagine the feeling of being unwanted, not being loved? I knew it at that moment. I needed my mother, my family...a husband ...somebody by my side, and there was nobody.

After a couple of weeks of emotional and physical suffering, the time finally came for the two of us to be released and the suffering to surrender to happiness. We were finally free to go home to our big sister who was waiting impatiently for the two of us.

It was time for me to accept this little creature without any reservations and time to put an end to all of our suffering. It was evident that God was going to give us more pain and more suffering and taught us life the hard way if we did not accept the gifts that he was offering.

This baby was sent to me as a special gift, and at times I was refusing it, so God made us both suffer until we realised that keeping healthy and being faithful to each other was the best thing we could do and that our sufferings would continue until we surrender to the family. We all have to learn to trust God, even if we do not understand his plan.

The other thing I've learned is that we should always listen to our hearts, not to everybody else. Otherwise, we will continue to suffer as we have an emotional reaction to everything that is said to us. Real power is in sitting back and observing things with logic. True power is resistant. If words control you, that means everything else can control you.

Breathe and allow the thing to pass. If I had continued on with my anger towards my husband, I would not have been able to hold on and raise my little one to be a charming, beautiful young lady. My marriage was like torture for a long period of time, and it ended with a nasty divorce, but each one of the hard days I would look at my girls, hug them, and thank God to have chosen me to be their mother.

As for my husband, he was always cold to the girls during our twenty years of marriage. I never saw him showing affection to them. Not even once had I seen him worrying when they had a temperature. He would spend most of his earnings on alcohol and gambling. His only time with the family would be the BBQ that he used to make very often, which we all really enjoyed. Looking back now from this perspective, my dolls loved that just because of the need to be loved by their father. It's the same thing that I was doing, surrounding myself and giving up my education, hobbies, and social life just to try to make things with the marriage work.

Life has taught me the hard way to let the moment pass before speaking. All the storms will pass through our lives, but we need to find a shelter made out of love and fight for it. All of us need to form that special bond with the new generation and learn how to nurture and love them.

The bird is nothing without it is a nest, and raising kids was my choice. I gave up things and went without them. I regret nothing. Never regret anything in life. What's meant to be will always be, and we all learn to not make the same mistakes again after these experiences.

My life was and will always be for my children, no matter how big they get. They did not ruin my life but gave me a whole new view of the meaning of life. There is nothing in this world that can break the bond of love between a mother and her children.

"**If you want light to come into your life, you need to stand where it is shining.**"

~ Guy Finley

CHAPTER SEVEN

A Pennsylvania Summer Day

By Andrea Daylor

It was a warm summer day in Pennsylvania. With every patio stone I skipped on, I would look up towards the sun and notice something: the sun was following me. The warmth covered my skin like a blanket, and I knew without a doubt that the sun wasn't ever going to stop following me. Many years later, I still look up to the skies to feel reassured that the sun is still following me. So much life has happened, the ups and downs, the wins the losses, and all the hundreds of lessons. And through it all, the sun still comes up every morning.

Life was pretty easy for me during my childhood. It wasn't until I had my first heartbreak in college that I realized the sun wasn't quite enough to bring the comfort it brought me when I was a little girl in my sundress, dancing on the patio out back. When I reached my twenties, I was diagnosed with depression and anxiety. It didn't make sense to me. I was always the strong one, the funny one, the smart one. I had it all, or at least I thought I did. How could I be depressed?

I was now entering my thirties with the grand title of being a divorced single parent. I felt like I was Ross, from the TV show

Friends! I had married my best friend right out of college. He was the kindest, funniest, most caring man I had ever met. He was the guy that made laugh so hard I couldn't breathe. He and his friends used to "shake the floors" of our old high school building. There's something about a nun bouncing right in front of you that will make you laugh until you literally can't catch your breath!

Jay had the same warmth as the sun. He was a best friend that held a candle to my dad, my hero. I adored him and everything about him. Jay moved with me to Florida from our hometown of Harrisburg, Pennsylvania to follow my snowbird parents and career at the time. Several years later, we were pregnant with our first child. Sadly, soon after, we realized we had grown apart. Even with the amount of love we had for one another and our baby boy, Bryce Kevin Baker, we decided it was best after five years of marriage to divorce and raise our son as friends. I lost my best friend, my hero, and my greatest asset. Life started to really show me how difficult it could be. Since then, Jay has found his true soulmate and she too has that warmth like the sun. They just make your heart full. It has been such a blessing watching Bryce grow into such a fine young man with them sharing being his parents. Just because you get divorced or change a relationship doesn't mean you can't be friends and be on the same team (especially for your child).

I knew after my divorce that I had to find someone to help me navigate these category five hurricanes that were swirling in my heart. I found her. She was a licensed mental health counselor in Ponte Vedra Beach, Florida. Little did I know at the time that this woman would be a great teacher of wisdom, faith, and healing. It was during a session discussing the grief of my divorce when God forced those words out of my mouth. I blurted something out that would never be undone. I hadn't planned it, and I had no idea what I said after I heard my own words. "I was sexually abused" came out of my very own lips. I was more taken back than my therapist was. I began vividly recalling being abused at a grocery store by a complete stranger when I was about six years old. This was the 1970s, so you never heard about children being abused or abducted. It happened...to me.

The Perfect Family and The Perfect World

My parents always had my four siblings and me dressed from head to toe without a hair out of place. We were the picture-perfect family, and I was surrounded by love, security, and clothed in outfits that always matched my three older brothers and younger sister. We laugh now at the endless pictures of matching plaid get-ups and Mary Jane shoes. This day of recollection though shattered my innocent childhood. I remember that day clearly. I had on a white lace halter top with pink ruffly shorts as I went along with my mom to the grocery store. I had decided in my stubborn little head that I was not about to go into the frozen section to freeze while my mom took forever to pick her perfect produce. So, I independently sat in the book section reading whatever interested me. I had no idea that evil was about to interrupt me.

An elderly man wearing dirty pants and a bright orange hunting jacket limped over to me and asked me to help him. I recall obliging reluctantly, knowing deep inside that something was wrong. Several minutes passed with him taking me wherever he could be alone with me in the store. He touched me everywhere, and I was changed forever. My perfect world with the sunshine always following me was stolen from me. There were terrible things in this world. It wasn't perfect anymore.

My heart raced and I couldn't think clearly. After about ten minutes, this man was brave enough to try to take me out of the store. (I have three older brothers that involuntarily taught me some serious wrestling moves)! I twisted my arm quickly and freed myself of his death grip on my wrist. I ran to my mom and told her what had happened. A kind man in the same aisle screamed for help. That bad man was never found, at least not by us. I forgave him, though.

A few years later, into my seemingly perfect childhood from a big, close, Italian Irish Catholic family, I was violated again. How could this happen twice? My brother's "friend" sexually abused me in the safety of my own home. My parents were upstairs, making sure everyone had breakfast, planning a fun Saturday. Meanwhile downstairs, the world showed me that evil still exists. What was I doing wrong? Why did I deserve this? How can bad things happen to good people? Again, my heart forgave. Instinct or fear, you don't tell anyone. You feel like it's your fault and that you are dirty.

Motherhood

Joy definitely entered my life with motherhood. But now, I had a divorce to heal from, as well as these horrible memories that were now surfacing. I had no idea why all of this was happening. Life seemed perfect before. I had the perfect son, the perfect career, the perfect family, and now I am divorced with dark secrets from my past. Who would want to hurt an innocent little girl? And why? And who has time to clean up messes from the past while trying to be a good parent and survive the hustle and bustle of today? Things just weren't making sense to me, so I worked extra hard at controlling my environment to be as perfect as can be. I had a great career and had the great income, I kept the house immaculate, kept in shape and made sure to always have fun with my pride and joy, Bryce and family. Brycey made my world complete. Life looked good on the outside. Inside I was hurt, and I was covering it up with all the things that money and looks could buy. It caught up with me, though. There was no more running from the abuse, my depression and anxiety, or the many mistakes I made. I was in pain.

Along came my forties. Hello, second divorce, and now single mother of two sons. Rowan Michael joined Bryce Kevin, and I knew I was the happiest mommy on the planet. Rowan brought even more joy to my heart. Even though we didn't have the fairytale family with the white picket fence like I planned my whole life, I was happy. There is absolutely nothing I love more than my sons, other than God. Being a single parent, though definitely came with struggles. During this trying time, I learned gratitude. I remember watching families that had their daddies with them, but I knew to look past that and soak in the beauty of nature. It always seemed to be a sunset that captivated me and forced me to breathe in the pink atmosphere with tons of gratitude. Even though my favorite star was leaving me for a bit, I learned to appreciate it while it was there.

The past kept getting in my head. I went to Bible studies, to confession and I finally told my parents of my incidences of sexual abuse as a child...I did everything I was supposed to do to right my wrongs. Why was I still hurting? Why did the tears come every time I wasn't with my sons or even when they fell asleep? I used to always pray with them and kiss them when I'd tuck them in and just watch them drift off to sleep. My heart would get heavy from letting go of another blessed day with them... even when they tried my last nerve! I wanted to give them the perfect world.

Why wasn't I able to keep either marriage together? I asked God what I was doing wrong and how to fix it. I had no one else to ask now, so I asked God. I admit, He was my last resort. And boy did He answer. One of my favorite verses is Philippians 4:13: "I can do all things through Christ who strengthens me." God was whispering to me to be strong. Sometimes He had to raise His voice so I would listen! I'm positive now that He planned it that way to get through my thick head! I started attending the Catholic church regularly and heeding every word out of the priests' mouths.

My parents always took us to church growing up. It was a way of life for me. I stopped going through the motions though and really listened to the messages. Bryce and I used to take our elderly neighbor with Alzheimer's to church with us. It just felt right, and it brought all of us joy. I became part of a Bible study with Father Kelly from St. Paul's at the beach. I got to sit and talk to this amazing and holy man about what the Bible meant. Even though I learned it all of my life, I wasn't ready to absorb it and live it as I did at this time. Huge difference. I was starting to really receive the Lord, clarity, and love for myself.

Things began to happen that I couldn't make Earthly sense of at the time. Even though life was sucker punching me, there were still these beautiful moments that stole my attention away from how hard life was getting. It was 2015 and I was newly separated from the love of my life with three sons now. Michael Nickas swept me off my feet, even though I tried to make sure he wouldn't. I first fell for his dad, who was the wittiest patient I'd ever had. I was a Regional Director of Rehabilitation, managing several therapy departments in different facilities throughout Northeast Florida. There was one facility that I frequented often as it was near my home. It also was the home of my favorite patient, Mr. Nickas. This Mr. Nickas had me wrapped around his finger and he knew it. He and I had our very own special relationship before I even met his family. One day he introduced me to this handsome man who happened to be his son! He said to his son, Michael, with the cutest Southern draw, "Michael, I want you to meet Andrea (even pronouncing my name the proper Italian way). "Isn't she beautiful? She's done gone through two husbands. This girl is trouble!" Great. So now, every time I saw Michael entering the facility, I would either hide or leave! I was too embarrassed and weak in the knees to face him! Two years later, I was engaged to Michael and giving birth to the most beautiful little boy, Anthony Michael Christopher Nickas. He entered the world in July of 2014, a year, precisely to the day, that his one of a kind grandfather left us.

Michael and I call Anthony our miracle. Anthony keeps Michael and I focused on what really matters. We continue to learn from our miracle. I gave birth to Anthony at 43 years of age. Michael and I wanted a child and prayed for God's will to be done. He was truly a gift and we knew it. My sons are my purpose as is serving others. Know your purpose. If you aren't sure what it is, be still and let the answer come to you. What makes you happy to be alive?

One day when Anthony was a baby, I drove home from work wishing that I could buy Anthony a water table that night.... yes, that night. I wanted it for my son's first birthday and had to have it. I cried during my late drive home that night, knowing that I couldn't get that present, nor would I be seeing Anthony on his first birthday. He was across the country, traveling with his father while I worked a rigorous management job. As I turned onto my neighborhood, a water table (in excellent condition) was sitting in the street next to a trash can. That table made it to my backyard! It and gave my sons and me hours of fun, splashing and relief on summer days in Florida. It may not seem like much to you, but how does the exact gift literally appear in your path minutes after you prayed for it? It came with such a gut feeling of being blessed that I can't capture the words to describe it.

I'll share another favorite God moment story with you. One day in Pennsylvania, my mother and I were visiting my grandfather, Pasquale Venturini, who passed away on May 22, 1989, the worst day of my life. He was my all-time favorite person. Whenever I go to the cemetery, I just talk away because I know they can hear me. This day, I was talking to him standing by the wall he was buried in and asked him to please send me money to go to 3B's so I can get ice cream. As my mom (my grandfather's daughter) and I were walking to her car, a 20-dollar bill danced in the wind across my feet. That would be a scoop of mint chocolate chip and a scoop of chocolate peanut butter ice cream for me! The sun halted above as I bent over to pick up the money. Thank you, grandpop. Even with him in Heaven, or should I say, especially with him in Heaven, I feel his love!

It was moments like those that started to add up. They usually came during pain and heartbreak, but they were part of this beautiful journey. Love became so real and resilient. We throw the word "love" around a lot. There is only one kind of love people. It is CORINTHIANS LOVE. "Love is patient. Love is kind. It does not envy. It does not boast. It does not dishonor others. It is not self-seeking, it is not easily angered, it keeps no record of wrongs. Love does not delight in evil but rejoices with the truth." Read that again. Seriously. How often do we get angered? How often do we boast? Nothing saddens me more than seeing people worship material things or work that is self-serving. If the payoff is material, is it really serving others? Do they not recognize time with their child or loved ones is so much more than a high-priced possession? It makes me feel empathy those around them that aren't being cherished the way God intended. It is great to want a vast territory and substantial income but is it your idol? Is it stealing who God meant you to be, including the parent you committed to being? Are their things that are distracting you from your children or purpose? I always think of Mother Theresa. She truly gave without her hand out. In my past, I climbed the corporate ladder and got the large paychecks, but I wasn't in alignment, even though we as therapists are helping others. It took my time and focus from my children. I could buy them things, but they didn't replace me. I have always said, "Bigger houses, bigger trash cans." I wanted to be home while I could and make messes with my kids. I wanted to be able to help my college student with a philosophy paper while creating the perfect dinner for my 13-year-old food critic and dance to Disney music with my toddler. And yes, all at the same time!! Time is too limited and so precious. I choose now to make time to dance whenever we can and wherever we can. When I see my sons dancing in public, I know I did something right! Be the person God intended you to be, not the person that human nature makes you think you need to be loved, Corinthians loved. You will be judged. We are only human and see what we want to see in others. My pastor, Spike Hogan preached to us to not fall into the gap between what you expect and what you receive. Fill that space with hope, faith and love instead of disappointment. It makes all the sense in the world! I have learned to be quick to forgive. I still shoot straight from the hip and will defend my territory but with a much more forgiving and loving heart..

I Found My Path

When I was in high school, pondering what I wanted to be when I grow up, I went to a college fair. I visited a booth that had a sign that said 'Occupational Therapy.' The woman at the booth explained the career to me as a medical position, much like being a nurse, but you don't just give pills to a patient. As much as I wanted to be a doctor, Occupational Therapy was "my thing". I didn't want to spend years in medical school. I wanted to be a mommy as soon as possible! With Occupational Therapy, you get to teach patients of all ages how to do for themselves after an accident or illness. You get to teach them how to do whatever they need to do to live a life of quality. Wait, what? I can help people live better lives? I can actually do something that helps other people and have fun doing it (and get paid well for it)? I have been an Occupational Therapist for over 20 years now and thank my parents every day for putting me through college. I was a little perturbed they wouldn't let their first daughter go to Pitt and chose a Catholic school for me, but I get it now! The same nun that taught me in kindergarten resided at my college's convent. Either it was karma or a pleasant surprise! I do know this: all things happen for a reason in life. This fact has given me new strength for handling the loss. Maybe God plans it that way so as we start to lose loved ones, like our parents, we are somewhat equipped to weather that astonishing loss. I am not sure how I will breathe when I have to endure that, but I know that God (and my parents) will be with me. Michael and I talk a lot about losing loved ones. He teaches me to be patient and cherish every day because when they are gone, they are gone forever.

I have met so many patients that have changed my life. Here my job was to help them, but they were teaching me. There were so many God moments that I had no idea were God moments at the time. Now when they happen, I simply say, "Thank you." A very dear patient of mine recommended a book. After telling me about the hit and run accident that took her son's life, she proceeded to tell me about the glorious life she has led. She amazed me. Someone took her son from her, yet she still enjoyed life. I saw the raw pain in her soul when she spoke of losing him, but she still found joy in each day. How? She had faith, relentless faith. My sons are the air I breathe. I'd suffocate without them. I often wonder if they will ever know how much I love them. How could someone survive to be ok without their child? The answer came to me before I left her home the day I met her. God. God is the only answer. I loved this woman for her strength and faith. My patient and I soon realized how much we enjoyed each other's company and how similarly we viewed life. She told me to get a book called 'Angels Among Us.' Within a week, I finished the book and was sending a message to the author, Clint Stanton, to thank him for sharing such a heartfelt and beautiful story. He tells the reader about the sweet memories with his mother, which included watching Forrest Gump on his last Mother's Day with her. Clint wrote about the feather that drifted by Forrest as he put his son with the love of his life, Jenny, on the bus. Minutes after I read that chapter, I went into our study and saw a white feather sitting on the sofa. I was so moved by this that I taped the feather to one of our coasters. I didn't want to forget the significance of that God moment. I now have copies of Clint Stanton's cd's and a t-shirt for my patient and me, personally sent from Clint himself. God is good.

The Best Instruction Book

I have learned so many lessons from my depression, anxiety, relationships, and abuse. There is one resounding lesson, though. The Bible is the best instruction book for life. Read that sentence again if you need to! Don't be so consumed with material things or social media that it distracts you from living a truly Godly life. The love of Money is the root of all evil. Yes, you should have it if it makes you happy, however, don't let it distract or confuse you from what really matters. Are you being an honest person, or are you walking a walk for your own gain? If you can't be honest with yourself, you won't know the power and peace of living a Godly life of abundance. And be kind. We all have a story but don't transfer your account onto someone else like I did. You will be hard pressed not to receive blessings if you live by the Ten Commandments and the Golden Rule. And let me be clear, I am far from perfect. I think Jesus knew I was coming along when he died for our sins! I wish I could personally apologize to every person I have ever hurt. I'd pay whatever consequences I could to take away any pain I have caused. But I cannot and I have three sons that I need to be amazing for. Instead of crying now when I watch them sleep, I smile and thank God for another day with them. Michael and I keep each other grounded and remind each other of what truly matters. We have learned from so many mistakes we have made. We have asked for God's healing and blessings upon our family. Make sure you have a best friend that shows you who you are and who you want to be. It may not always be pretty but make sure to be honest with yourself.

My older brother Chris always tells me to "Keep the main thing." He and I know what that means when we text KTMT. Keep the main thing in life. Follow life's instruction book.

Follow the 10 Commandments! One of the key lessons I needed to learn was to love myself. We hear that all the time, maybe so much so that we have lost the value in those words. Eat right, exercise, limit or avoid toxins, get your sleep, surround yourself with things that make you happy. The times I couldn't afford flowers (but realized the sight of them made me happy) I would pick them from outside. Drive safely, live in the moment, slow down, recognize that everyone has a story. If you feel sad, feel it then move on. Find the positive things in life. Don't rush to judge but know when to remove people, places, or things in your life that are toxins for you. We are all different with different tastes. Variety is the spice of life! As for me, I have created my own health and wellness business that provides me the comfort of being a mommy and serving others. I roll with the punches now and thank God for the challenges. I hold onto the friendships that bring me joy and help me grow. I see the sunshine in everything.

Our time here on Earth is like a grain of sand. Our human bodies can only process so much mentally and physically. Have the peace of mind to know and accept that there is something so much greater than we. Fill your mind with good messages. I listen to a Christian radio station and nothing makes me happier than hearing my sons sing, "I Can Only Imagine." Breathe in love and exhale gratitude. Respect that we are not in control of the universe. Maximize what you can do as a human being and find the joys and blessings in even difficult times. Live in alignment and give positive energy to others. If you open up your mind, arms and heart to receiving God, love and sunshine, it will find you. Keep the main thing. The sun will follow you, I promise. You just have to look up.

> "In the end, it's all worth it. The pain behind your smile, the struggles behind your success and the past behind your present."
>
> ~ Saksham Vyas

CHAPTER EIGHT

A Guide to Liberate Your Struggle Through Authentic Transformation

By Anastasia Gunawan

Throughout my life, I have experienced many moments of synchronicity. Synchronicity is a natural phenomenon that occurs within the scope of human experience. It is often made up of seemingly coincidental events or cues that hold a powerful and often personal meaning to the observer. Very recent synchronicity in my life led me to John Spender and *A Journey of Riches*. This chapter represents experiences of my own personal journey of riches. Every space between words is filled with gratitude. I will be forever grateful to have had the opportunity to share my truth with the world.

A few years ago, I completed graduate school to become a social epidemiologist. Social epidemiologists are scientists who study the effects of social-structural factors related to the health of the human population. We study the distribution of advantages and disadvantages in society and how they are associated to human health and disease. For example, children who are born into poverty, and have adverse childhood experiences of abuse and neglect are more likely to exhibit unhealthy behaviors later in life. This finding led to the development of Adverse Childhood Experience (ACE) score. Individuals with a higher ACE score are at higher risk for developing certain physical diseases and social and emotional problems. One prominent study in the United States that investigates ACE is The CDC-Kaiser Permanente Adverse Childhood Experiences (ACE) Study (Visit https://cdc.gov for more information).

I was fascinated with the study of health from a sociological perspective because of my upbringing. Growing up, I was raised in a single-parent household. My mother is a piano teacher who is also a brilliant musical performer. I would describe her as a very passionate woman. My sister and I relied on my mother's earned income to make ends meet, teaching children how to play the piano. The three of us lived in a one-bedroom duplex in a quiet neighborhood near city college.

I am also from a family of immigrants so English is my second language. The United States of America used to be a foreign country 8,000 miles across the Pacific Ocean from my birth country, Indonesia. After years of residence in the U.S., it eventually began to feel like home. It is not a foreign country to me anymore, but that sense of familiarity and belonging took some time to develop.

As an immigrant child, I didn't overthink my circumstances. I didn't compare my life to other kids. In high school, I was focused on fulfilling my dream to attend college. I remember how passionate I was about what would be possible if I attended college so I earned good grades in my classes, participated in clubs/organizations (orchestra, ROTC, Academic Olympics Club), and worked my way to varsity member of the rifle team. My high school days were filled with activities that I really enjoyed. I thought, 'If high school is this fun, I can't even imagine how fun college will be!'

One day, I was sitting in my third period trigonometry class when my teacher received a note instructing me to visit the Guidance Counselor's office. As I walked down the hallway, I wondered what this was going to be about. Was I in trouble?

I waited outside of the office as I did at the beginning of my senior year, I gave myself an important mission, applying for as many scholarships as I could. This was a critical mission because I couldn't afford to pay my college tuition on my own. I submitted multiple scholarship applications throughout the semesters and prayed every night that they would be accepted. Four months before my high school graduation watched other students coming and going. Eventually, my counselor called my name to enter his office and he asked me to take a seat. My palms were sweaty and I couldn't help feeling anxious. I watched him pick up a red portfolio folder, and as he opened it, he turned to face me and said, "Congratulations, Anastasia. The scholarship committee came to an agreement to award you with full-ride tuition to the university." I took a long pause and my eyes swelled up with tears of disbelief. I felt like I was dreaming.

Synchronicity often plays out unexpectedly. There is no telling when, where, or how it will unfold. My experience with synchronicity has helped me understand a pearl of wisdom about life: I cannot change the circumstances that the universe has orchestrated for me. I couldn't change my financial circumstances at the time that left me unable to afford college but my choices and actions matter more than my struggles. My deliberate actions to succeed, and aligning those actions with my dream of attending college led me to that exact moment of meeting with my counselor. I was able to manifest and witness the fulfillment of my desire because I had acted in a manner that served my dreams and created possibilities without doubt or limitations resulting from my current circumstances.

From my experience as a young teen, I learned how to minimize my struggle psychologically. I developed a habit of not carrying my struggles into my daily routine. I earned good grades in all my classes and studied for the SAT and ACT college entrance exams even though I did not know if I would even be able to attend college. I was preparing for my dream against some apparent odds.

As a little girl, I enjoyed spending time sketching home interior designs and apparel. I would role play of owning my own design business with fake clients. Throughout my childhood, I accumulated stacks of business portfolios and sketches as a result of my unreserved creativity and imagination. As I got older, I started yearning for greater purpose and meaning, asking myself, "Who do I want to be? How can I contribute to this world?"

It became apparent after conducting my own research and projecting my younger self into the future that I would not find personal fulfillment designing clothes or creating beautiful homes for myself or other people. Through trial and error, I eventually found my way to the health sciences. Health sciences offer countless career opportunities to serve others. This field provided a solution for my relentless yearning for greater meaning and purpose that is bigger than myself. With that pursuit in mind, I chose to study Neuroscience in college. I developed a curiosity for the human brain and the dynamics of internal and external variables in life that influence human behavior. The decision to pursue a career in this field came to me as a surprise, considering my childhood passion for the creative arts.

My full-ride scholarship to college gave me boundless freedom to fuel my curiosity. I learned how to cultivate and access intelligence effortlessly. I watched other college students struggle in classes, choosing the right degree and feeling uneasy about the direction of their path. I did not understand why it was a big struggle for many. I have always trusted my intuition and curiosity to guide me. There are times when I fear my own intuition because it may seem irrational or illogical, but when it comes to making the big decisions in my life, I trust it entirely because being receptive to your intuition can help guide you to a life of ease.

The opposite of ease is disease. As a public health professional, I see disease and human suffering in an array of complex cause and effect models. Shortly after my college graduation, I decided to take a year off before pursuing graduate school. The primary driving force behind my post-graduate life was ambition. I wanted to DO more. I wanted to BE more. This ambition carried me through the next phase of my life.

I applied to a local public health graduate training program despite not having any idea how I would be able to pay for it. A few weeks after submitting my application, I received an opportunity to accept financial assistance from the program. My tuition would nearly be free with the opportunity to earn extra money by working with an assigned mentor in my selected field of study. It was a chance to network and learn from an experienced group of researchers and scientists. A week prior to starting my graduate program, I had accepted an on-call organ recovery technician position at a local hospital in addition to my graduate program and research projects. I worked over 50 hours a week for the next two years.

Halfway through my training, I started to feel the pressure from myself and others around me to excel in research. I had multiple incidents of unexplained skin rashes, temporary loss of consciousness, and weight gain. I completely disregarded these symptoms as being potentially life-threatening. My intuition told me I was experiencing symptoms of burning out but I wanted to save lives and pursue good work. I was receptive to my intuition but did not act on it this time.
I wanted to be a superhero for others, but I completely neglected myself in the process and became a burned-out byproduct of my ambition. When I finally graduated, my family and loved ones attended my graduation celebration. I felt so much love, pride, and success but it was a fleeting moment that came with a debilitating cost from not listening to my intuition. From the outside looking in, I was on the path to success; however, at the peak of my success, I felt utterly powerless. I was struggling with poor health, negative body image, a break-up from a seven-year relationship with someone whom I cared for deeply, and sadness and grief that filled every minute of my waking life. Our lives are filled with hidden lessons. I spent a few years after my training searching for whys. Why did I fail to see this burn-out coming? Why do I feel so powerless? I started to write down events that happened from my past, dissecting them objectively.

As I started to dissect my past experiences on paper, I realized a lot of things that I needed to change. The first thing I realized that needed a tune-up in my life was my diet. My diet was predominantly refined carbohydrates that are commonly found in white flour, white bread, white rice, pastries, sodas, snacks, pasta, sweets, breakfast cereals, and added sugars. I had a very minimal intake of fruit and vegetables. At the time, my diet did not support my life and goals. I did not know how much processed food I was eating until my health started to decline. I love to use the excuse of not having enough time to prepare nutritious foods that my body will love but it was a costly excuse because my poor dietary choices definitely contributed to my burn-out.

According to World Health Organization, burnout is a legitimate medical diagnosis. It is not something to be proud of — to admit to myself and others that at 23 years old, I had already experienced burn-out. I was experiencing low energy, mood swing, migraines, and skin rashes. It was quite shocking to me because I never planned to experience these health symptoms so early in my life. In hindsight, every life experience carries a lesson.

My experience with chronic disease taught me to always put my body and health as my number one priority in life. I learned to do this by taking small steps. I signed up for a gym membership with one of my best friends. I was committed to doing cardio and weight exercises at least three times a week. I became more deliberate in my food selection and purchasing only healthy foods. I started to incorporate more vegetables, fruits, fiber, fish, and nuts into my diet. Once my small steps became a daily routine, I started feeling healthier and stronger. I was not easily stressed or irritated. I was no longer experiencing migraines. I felt stronger, joyful, and happier than ever before.

Transformation requires a healthy dose of commitment and dedication. Healthy eating habits liberated me from symptoms of chronic disease. My journey to clean eating inspired me to take the time to select, prepare, and cook foods that feed my body and soul. I fell in love with cooking for myself and others on my journey of clean eating.

In my search, I found a profound lesson that there's a distinction between taking inspired action versus uninspired action. To live a truly authentic, successful life, I needed to start taking inspired action. My struggle in the past stemmed from my inability to discern the difference between inspired and uninspired actions that led me to disease and feeling powerless. Taking inspired action can lead you to a happier, more fulfilled and joyful state of being. In the past, I had failed to take control of my own life. It led to the development of habitual negative coping mechanisms that continued until I hit rock bottom. I had my share of illnesses and decreased quality of life due to my unchecked ambitions. I was an emotional eater, addicted to my ambition. If I hadn't have hit rock bottom, I would have continued living on autopilot with harmful coping mechanisms. Negative coping mechanisms were undoubtedly adding negative cycles to my daily struggles.

Today, I have a healthy relationship with food and myself. I learned how to access my personal power to take back my life. I enjoy accessing personal power through passion exercises, which is a fun process that gives me a direct route to my inner source of energy, confidence, and strength. Passion exercises are unique for every person. They are personal and can be identified through a series of trials and errors. I created a list of activities that I love and enjoy, and activities that I've not yet tried. I commit to one or two activities from each list per week to fuel my mind, body, and soul. I've been able to identify sources of inner power through outdoor activities from my list. I have a new-found love for hiking, paddle-boarding, and cycling. From this list, I've also identified that I'm an extrovert. Extrovert individuals tend to be outgoing and feel energized when they are around other people. I am an extrovert that is empowered when I'm in a conversation and working with others. As much as I love to engage with others, it was also important to develop a self-care routine because it serves as my personal relaxation guide during stressful times. I enjoy repeating affirmations, journaling, cooking, and doing yoga as my self-care routine activities.

Navigating this time of personal discovery was not always smooth sailing. I was entering a new romantic relationship, job hunting, and was dealing with a traumatic incident of attempted home burglary by a drug addict while I was taking a nap in my bedroom. These events left plenty of space for anxiety, stress, and the unknown. Accessing my personal power through passion exercises transformed me into a powerful, whole, and blissed-out human, capable of overcoming all of the life struggles thrown at me. I repeat the affirmation "I am more powerful than my struggles" when I catch myself focusing my energy on my struggles. Unconsciously, we give away our energy to our unwanted thoughts or circumstances. When I catch myself drifting away, I reaffirm that I am a powerful human being, and I choose to focus on my passion exercises. Optimal health and emotional well-being are sources of vitality, strength, and happiness. Regular exercise and balanced nutrition are key to optimal health. Working out releases dopamine, endorphins, and other neurochemicals for happiness, such as adrenaline, endocannabinoids, serotonin, and gamma-aminobutyric acid (GABA) for my body.

My personal journey to good health and positive body image required a lot of trial and error. I found that high-intensity interval and endurance training was most effective for my body. When it comes to nutrition, my body's inflammatory response is more balanced with a plant-based diet. I'm also incredibly grateful to have met some amazing friends through a company called Isagenix®. Isagenix® helped me gained optimal health in ways that otherwise would've taken me a long time to achieve. I was able to resolve issues with my allergies, skin rashes, and weight-gain thanks to living a plant-based lifestyle. Achieving optimal health costs money, time, and dedication, but the rewards are worth the investment.

When I'm out in the world, I also find joy through giving. Human beings are wired to feel useful in the spirit of service. Giving to the world around us requires one to cultivate our talents and gifts. We use gifts, money, time, words of encouragement, and many other skills for the purpose of empowering others. Giving in the spirit of service is hard-wired into our DNA. I also enjoy mentoring young high school and college students in my community. I serve as a mentor for a local group of women who are interested in pursuing science, technology, engineering, and mathematics (STEM). I set aside time every month to connect students interested in STEM to employers and local industries in my community. When I'm not mentoring women in STEM, I'm also passionate about developing programs for health promotion and education at a local state association group. Volunteering my time to a help others gives me so much joy!

Emotional well-being is equally as important as physical well-being. I incorporate affirmations in my morning meditation which helps frame my subconscious to be ready for all the things that I may experience that day. I repeat "I love myself (inhale), I'm thankful for...[fill in the blank] (exhale)." I set a timer and repeat this meditation exercise for seven minutes. I adopted my meditation exercises from Kamal Ravikant, author of *Love Yourself Like Your Life Depends On It*. He was the person who introduced me to the "I love myself" affirmation. I've modified it to include gratitude with each exhale because life is so magical. Each exhale serves as a token of appreciation for an unlimited supply of oxygen that fills my lungs so that I can thrive in life, despite my struggles. A thankful heart really does help you develop positive emotions that act as a protection shield from pain, anxiety, and fear caused by life's struggles. A thankful heart supports you on your journey of becoming a whole, healthy human being.

I'm also very thankful to have strong community support. Communities are built by people who share common ideas. Another part of overcoming your struggles in life is finding your community. To do this, you can list the things you value and even use your passion exercises list as a start. For example, I really love yoga. I connected with my local yoga community and have met so many wonderful people. Connecting with other people who dedicate their time living a passion that is similar to yours is a massive gift. Participate in a community that shares and builds their lives around passions and values that you love. Life is a journey of seeking, finding, enjoying, and letting go. At first, I was very nervous about going out and building new relationships after completing my passion exercises. I am grateful to myself for not staying in my comfort zone. I'm so high on life from the authentic relationships that I've built as a direct result.

What is holding you back from reaching out to others? What are some of the voices in your head that stop you from building that next connection or friendship? I had to confront these questions for myself to eliminate any feelings of doubt, fear, and insecurity. Once you're connected with a community – friends, colleagues, acquaintances, support groups – don't be afraid to be open and vulnerable with them. Insecurity was one of the first voices I had to confront in my quest to build new, authentic relationships. Once you've identified them, dissect them until they're no longer an obstacle. Be fearless and creative when developing your own personal guide on how to thrive – not merely survive – as a human being.

We are not immune to struggles in life. There will be struggles that we are prepared for, and others we are not. It does require time and effort to cultivate authentic inner power, but my hope is that my story will guide you to your own unique, authentic, personal transformation, so you are always ready to face your struggles as a powerful and whole being.

Allow your cup to runneth over!

"Once all struggle is grasped, miracles are possible."

~ Mao Zedong

CHAPTER NINE

LIFE IS CHANGE

By Lillian Tahuri

"Holy shit what have I done now!", I said to myself as I walked out of Kabul International Airport taking in the unfamiliar sights of men in uniforms carrying weapons, and others in all manner of traditional and western clothes. Unusual sights were accompanied by unfamiliar sounds: the noise of a continual stream of large aircraft arriving and departing; military and UN helicopters with their low rhythmical *chuf chuf chuf* buzzed overhead. Children were waiting to carry my bag for a coin and military personnel tried to give me directions to the pick-up point outside the airport perimeter. They did a great job, their determination prevented me from wandering into restricted areas.

As I continued the long walk to the pick-up point gripping my long dark canvas bag, I was thinking that it would not have been a good idea to bring my pink, wheeled luggage set, which would have got damaged on the uneven surfaces. More importantly, I knew my self-talk line was the signal that a new adventure had just commenced, a new book without a beginning or an end, and I was confidently walking into it.

As planned, the security team were there, ready, efficient and swift.

Although I had been on many adventures before, this one was different. I was walking out of my old life, having left home with no plans to return. I had resigned from my job of nine years, my young adult children were living their own lives, and the cats went with them.

Freedom.

Before my arrival in Afghanistan, I was a single working mother bringing up my children as the primary parent taking care of their everyday needs. As most mothers will tell you, there is no better role in life than raising children, nothing else comes close.

With family comes responsibility. As a mother, everyone else's needs come first. I was no exception. I now call this TMS (the mother syndrome) because, as a transformational leader, nearly all mothers I have worked with have put everyone else first, they have not taken care of their own needs, they don't feel that they can spend money or time on themselves, they even feel guilty thinking about taking personal time. This state of putting everyone else first can go on for years even after their children have left home.

I was the sole person responsible for my children's wellbeing and I worried that if I didn't work hard enough, get better educated and move along a career pathway then my family would suffer and they wouldn't have the life I envisaged for them. As a consequence, I found myself in a cycle lasting many years, where I worked too hard, completed a university degree while working full time, all the while making sure I never missed any sporting, school or community event.

I am a Maori, raised in Aotearoa, New Zealand. Maoris are brought up with a set of cultural values that include *whanaungatanga* (the importance of family and extended family) and *manaakitanga* (the importance of caring for everyone). These values become a part of who we are and drive our need to take care of everyone. It was my cultural values, commitment and obligation that set me on a 17-year long journey representing our tribe in an historical grievance process that ended in a multi-million-dollar settlement. That was how I became stuck in a comfortable rut. I had reached a point where I was comfortable in my career, I was satisfied with my education, and my little family was doing well. It dawned on me that life was comfortable for everyone around me, but not for myself. I had not taken care of my wishes and desires for my own life.

You can't change your life without doing anything differently, right? I started on a journey of personal development and stumbled across Stephen Covey's *The Seven Habits of Highly Successful People*. This book, and the activities contained in it, helped me to prioritise what was important to me, to make plans and to schedule those plans. It assisted me in sorting out and achieving short, medium, and long-term goals. Not only was I smashing my goals each year, I was also resetting them!

The *Seven Habits* method was highly successful for me. Not only is it a great prioritising and planning tool, it has an excellent moral compass embedded in its design. I was able to achieve more in a shorter space of time than I had without this method, it was both efficient and effective. I was still caring for my family as a priority, but I was now taking care of myself as well. The only problem was ... I took it a little too far, I was constantly exhausted, thinking I needed to do it all and have it all. In other words, I was trying to be superwoman.

It was at about this time that my sister took me along to a Chris Howard event, which started another journey whereby I became a master NLP practitioner and a master hypnotist. These gave me insights into new tools and techniques to transform my life, and the lives of others, at a far deeper level.

The underlying core beliefs and patterns of behaviours that have been imprinted in us from the day we are born, through our experiences in this world, and from people in our lives mould us into the people we become. This is the lens through which we see the world and we make decisions from this perspective. Growing up, we were exposed to many cultures and religions with their multitude of gods and demi-gods. This was a world which we moved in and out of freely. As we got older, we realised that many religions espoused themselves as the one and only true religion and saw themselves as superior to all others, and above the indigenous world view. We witnessed the limited point of views of parents as they argued which church or school their children would go to, each vying for their own choice.

This leads me to how I ended up in Kabul working in a private security company that, as a general rule, only hired former military or police personnel. I fell into neither of these categories. I used NLP tools to change my life at the unconscious level, the place where our core beliefs live and drive our behaviours. The NLP processes helped me eliminate the core beliefs that were holding me back or stopping me from progressing. Then I used these tools to set goals for the future, knowing that they would occur. And this is where I went a little off track.

I had intended to leave my comfortable rut to live and work in an unfamiliar place with a different culture and language. I wanted to up my game, challenge myself and do something completely different while utilising my past experiences. With all this in mind, I completed a future goal setting process, but without a particular destination in mind. Within weeks of going through this process, I walked into my boss's office and told her I was resigning with two weeks' notice, because I needed to be in Dubai for training, tests and then travel to Afghanistan. I promised her I would complete any of my outstanding tasks within that timeframe, leave full handover notes, and delegate different parts of my job to my staff until they could find my replacement.

My advice when engaging in transformational goal setting processes is this: be specific because you could end up in a country you didn't plan on, be careful what you wish for because you will get it, and go with the flow no matter what because new experiences can be challenging, and exciting! Life is a journey that should be lived to its full potential and beyond.

The last two weeks at my job was a learning experience in itself. I observed the full range of emotions that my colleagues experienced as a result of my decision to leave one of the most peaceful and secure countries in the world, to move to a country in conflict and which was notably corrupt. Some genuinely feared for my safety, some were excited about the opportunities I would have, while others perhaps wished it was them as they wondered how they could go about making changes in their own lives. This mirrored some of my old beliefs that had held me back from moving out of my comfortable rut, the old limiting beliefs that I had obliterated and exchanged for new resources to support me in the future.

By the time I had completed the year-long contract in Afghanistan, I was ready for another challenge. This was my opportunity to start again and reinvent myself, my life was a blank sheet of paper. It was time to revisit my values and align my life to these values. Family is essential to me and is one of my top values and that is why I make the effort to visit my children at least every three months even though they reside in a different country. While placing family at the top of my hierarchy, I also felt a growing desire inside me to assist people suffering from trauma.

Reflecting on my time in Afghanistan, one thing I know for sure and what I would like to share, is that you can change your current situation at any point in your life. You simply decide how you want to live and create that lifestyle. Whether you feel stuck in a job, a life of living other people's expectations or whether your mindset is keeping you locked into your own expectations built on society's norms, you can change. We are ultimately responsible for ourselves, our decisions and the consequences of them. There are no rules, yet most of us carry on doing the same thing day after day, year after year.

Since the desire to work with trauma victims first manifested itself, I have worked with hundreds of men and women using transformation techniques. Initially I started working with men because of my personal experiences, then I focused on women. People came to me through word of mouth, either because I had worked with someone they knew, or, they had heard about me through others. This suited my lifestyle as I was the one person with the time and the passion to help them address their trauma.

Generally, I have found that people came to see me for a particular reason but more often than not, the underlying issue was something very different than the outward manifestation of their traumatic experience. As we progressed through a session, it took a natural course to the place we needed to be. The transformation techniques create quick and effective change; sometimes, I wondered if the techniques were too good! A young man in his mid-twenties was given my name and I agreed to work with him. He was unable to approach young women for dates and was worried he would waste his youth without meeting anyone. Not long after working with him, he phoned me to say he was now on Tinder, a serial dater, having fun and meeting lots of nice young women. My older-person conservative self-talk reaction was, "Oh no, what have I assisted in creating?."

Then he went on to say, "I'm not sleeping with them. I'm just enjoying talking to women because I've never been able to do that." Whew! Eight months later, he phoned me to say he had found The One.

An older woman contacted me - I had previously worked with her daughter. She had lost her 24-year-old son to suicide two years earlier and had not moved forward from her grief. She then became involved in a violent relationship. At the end of our session, she told me it was the first time since her son's death that she was able to speak his name. This was really emotional for her and for me as well. She now talks freely about her son, has left the violent relationship, and has moved to another part of the country.

I agreed to work with a young woman that was introduced to me through a third party. I was told she was being restructured out of the job that she loved, she felt rejected and hurt and, naturally, was worried about her future. But, as it turned out, she wasn't primarily concerned about her employment status. She had been a type 1 diabetic her whole life and feared having a baby because of the medical risks. She had been unable to fall pregnant. Medical tests indicated that both her, and her partner, were physically fine. The fear of pregnancy was profoundly ingrained in this young woman, but at the same she was determined to overcome this fear, and this is what we worked on. Months later, I was fortunate enough to be taken to the hospital to meet her new baby boy. Mum, dad, and baby were all healthy and happy!

A woman in her 50s approached me, she had been in a 30-year marriage and her husband had had an affair. She only found out about the affair because their daughter accidently discovered text messages on his phone. Fast forward a year, acknowledging that she would have ups and downs every now again, she is now well and truly moving into her new life, happy at the opportunity to reinvent herself. After losing 30kgs, she now feels the freedom to follow one of her dreams and is well on her way to becoming a competitive body sculptor!

These anecdotes about individuals I have worked with are not just stories about their personal transformations, their courage to be willing and open to allow change to occur. They are stories that show whatever you have been through, are going through or think about what may happen in the future, you can take steps to change your outcome. Everyone has a story and everyone can change their story like these individuals that I have worked with.

One final story to leave with you – one of my passions is travelling and it is not uncommon for me wander around foreign places on my own. On one such adventure I found myself in Phnom Penh, then out of nowhere, I was hit hard and fast on the side of my body by a white car. I remember this because I saw it continuing its journey while the force of the impact had lifted me off my feet and up into the air. This is when I had the most surreal experience of my life! My brain quickly processed what had happened. I knew I was going to land hard on the side of the road and I didn't want to hit my head so my mind swiftly reminded me to break my fall as I had learned in judo many years earlier. As a consequence of that lightening decision, I saved myself from damage to my head, which could have been very serious. I did end up with cuts, grazes and bruises along the entire length of my arm, which had taken most of the impact. That was not the only lightening decision I had made in those seconds, my NLP training about trauma and phobias, and how they come into existence, also flashed through my mind. I decided I did not want that, so by the time I hit the ground, I had reframed the whole incident to ensure that I would not get any phobias or suffer trauma from this event. The outcome of this split-second decision to focus on falling correctly and to reframe the accident was that I do not have any phobias and I have not suffered trauma as a consequence of this event. Now, when I look back at this event or tell others about it, it is not because I have any feelings of negative emotion or signs of trauma, it is merely from the perspective of a storyteller.

I am truly grateful for the NLP training that enabled me to control my state of mind so that I could create a positive outcome even though the situation seemed very bleak indeed. I am grateful to my single mother who had the energy to find the resources to send me to judo week after week and, after all these years, the judo technique of breaking a fall came to me spontaneously.

The point of this little story is to remind us that, as humans, we attach meaning to events or so-called signs that happen in our lives. Sometimes when we continue to have bad events happen in our lives we may think that it is time to take a different direction, or it's time to pay attention to the details, we may even think that someone is trying to send a message. Then forever after, every time a negative event occurs, we take it as a time to change direction or course.

In this event I decided not to attach any meaning or feeling to the accident so that I would not anchor this event into any behaviour like crossing busy roads, or fear of vehicles, or label it the travel adventure from hell.

As a takeaway, I encourage you to notice whenever you get a sign, reframe it to what you want to achieve, give it a positive feeling and meaning and take that forward in your life.

I have thought a lot about passion and purpose. Many of the current lifestyle coaches and gurus sell you the story that you need to find your passion or purpose to be happy and to live the life of your dreams. Furthermore, they tell you if you do that, then you will have unlimited wealth. You see these stories on your social media feed and you hear success stories from people who have chosen to find their passion or purpose. Yes, I agree this can be the path for some, but it is not the only path. I have seen many people, including my own friends and family members, believing that this is the way, the truth and the life! Later they end up extremely disappointed after having spent hundreds of hours working on a project and having invested thousands of dollars in trying to achieve the expected results.

I did a little exercise to find my life's passion and purpose and quickly realised that this approach was too restrictive and prescriptive. It was counterintuitive to who I was as a person and how I love living my life. One of my passions and purposes was limiting and opposite to one of my core values … freedom. The notion of having a passion and a purpose was someone else's belief that they were selling. Wealth and quantification of wealth are different for everyone. Wealth for some is large amounts of money, for others it could mean their needs are provided for and they are free to pursue their dreams. Do the numbers and figure out how much you really need to live the life of your dream, it may be a lot smaller than the millions promised by the life coaches and gurus.

There are no rules, what works for one person may not necessarily work for you. If you find a formula that works for you, go ahead, go for it. If it doesn't, take the best of what you learn and make your own decisions and set your own direction. What are your values? Let them guide you. What are your core beliefs? If they are working for you, carry on. If your values are not working for you and getting in the way, get rid of them. Once you are free of negative beliefs, self-talk and behaviours, your mind will be open to exploring what truly lights your fire. You know what, you may find you have many passions that you want to try out. You may discover you have a sense of purpose in a particular area and you can pursue that with focused energy and vigour. Whatever you do remember, there are no rules, don't take on other people's beliefs and values, find your own. Have the courage to go forward and honour what is in your heart.

Start dreaming, then get out there, have fun, be curious and be courageous when trying new things. The only person that's stopping you is you! Yes, on a practical level it may be time and money stopping you, solve the problem and just do it. There are no guarantees that this day is not our last, remember this and act as if every day is your last. What do you want to fill your life with?

Listen to the wise ones that carry the ancient wisdom within them. These people surround you, but if you don't listen, you won't discover them. I have been fortunate to be amongst wise ones while leading our tribal negotiations against our government. They gave me unrelenting support to negotiate hard, they provided me with guidance at strategic moments and showed me the truth.

Today we see images around us in marketing and social media of happy people being successful. These images are deceiving and never tell the whole truth about a person, but nevertheless many people take them as valid and compare their ordinary lives with them. The reality is we're not always happy, smiling, and successful people all the time. Remember, it is okay to be hurt, angry, frustrated, and to feel like a failure. We all have moments of self-doubt and negative thoughts. However, don't stay there, confront any negative feelings you have head-on, change your state to feel confident, happy, or whatever you want to be. You are in control of your emotions; you just need to decide how you want to show up in the world.

As we move through life, we become bored, we are no longer growing or feeling alive. We are comfortable going through the motions doing what we did last year and the year before that. We lose courage to try new things and embark on new adventures. We may even be acting out our passions and priorities from years earlier, even though they are no longer fulfilling. Every year I revisit my passions and preferences and check that they are still relevant in my current circumstances. Some I carry over, some I stop, and some are completed so it's time to set new goals.

Many many years ago, when I reviewed my passions and priorities, I added one. I wanted to use my current knowledge, skills and relationships to represent my tribe. This became my focus. This became my reality. Then, in the following years, I realised I was carrying a lot of tribal knowledge and so I increased my goal ... I wanted to become one of our negotiators; then this became my reality. Representing our tribe has been a commitment over many years and has led to a successful outcome. As it takes a village to raise a child, it also takes a supportive tribe to support you as their representative. Even contributing to my tribe was driven by passion, it was not a journey I undertook alone, everyone contributed. I was the trusted mouthpiece at that time for my tribe.

It was a sad moment to see these goals leave my plan after many years, but on the other hand, it meant I was now able to move into the next stage of my life's journey with new goals. Life is too short; there are so many exciting things to fill it with. Be adaptable, be flexible and know that life changes whether we want it to or not, go with the flow into every stage with peace and ease to create your beautiful life.

As I write this chapter I am aware that my life and priorities are changing, some current goals are coming to an end, new passions have already entered that have given me opportunities that I never expected. In addition to that, I am now committed to a bigger long-term goal thats time has arrived. Embrace change and go with the flow.

Use everything you've got and more to achieve your dreams. It begins from the inside, find out who you are, what makes you tick, your values, what you love doing, what makes your heart sing. Undertake personal development with an open mind and an open heart. Be courageous when coming up against old hurts or failures, see them for what they are and move forward. When you feel like you are not progressing, notice the fear and challenges stopping you. Eliminate them at the unconscious level and carry on.

Trust that you can achieve what you want in life, seek guidance when you need it, but make your own decisions. Prioritise, plan and take action on what is most important to you first. Life is too short, only focus on the most meaningful passions that make you feel alive.

As I come to the closing paragraphs, I write confidently knowing that you will achieve what is important to you. I know this because on many occasions I have achieved even more than what I set out to achieve. From growing up in a small rural town in New Zealand, I have travelled to many countries. I was fortunate enough to represent my tribe in a multi-million-dollar historical settlement that will benefit our people for generations to come. With the skills of NLP, hypnosis and neuroscientific personal development that I've learned on my journey, I have been able to help both men and women transform their lives.

As you read my words, you will recall many achievements, big and small of your own. Knowing this, you will understand that dreams are achievable and they do become a reality.

Now go, dream of a bright future, the one that you see, feel and design in your mind's eye. See it coming to life in technicolour, feel the energy vibrating throughout your body and notice how daringly exciting it is perched on the edge of your future. Go out into the world with confidence, knowing that your dream will become a reality.

Make a plan, take action and move forward toward your dream. Look back every now and again to appreciate how far you have travelled, feel your achievements, smile from your soul, then set your eyes north again toward the future. Enjoy your journey in this life, relax and delight in the unexpected. It is the unexpected moments that give us great pleasure when we tell our stories. They become the experiences, knowledge and wisdom that we will share throughout our lives.

Always do what is important to you first. For me it is family, for others it could be health, travel or a hobby they are passionately obsessed with. You don't want to be the couple who work all their lives for the big overseas trip of a lifetime when they retire, then when that time comes, one of both are no longer fit or healthy enough to travel. Happiness is really important, whatever that means to you, do that.

Love and light.

"Never regret anything that has happened in your life, it cannot be changed, undone or forgotten. So take it as a lesson learned and move on."

~ Unknown

CHAPTER TEN

RISING ABOVE THE TIDE

By Jason Stein

In my chapter, I'm sharing several short stories that cover different time periods and experiences in my life, like different slices of the pie, so to speak. I've learned over the years that how we look at things makes a difference. So maybe some of these stories will resonate with you more than others, perhaps some will help you look at things differently. In any case, enjoy and hopefully, it's not too much of a struggle to get through them.

I've heard that struggling helps build character. But who wants to be constantly building their character? It sounds exhausting, right? The truth is, it can be, at times; but know that through the struggle comes progress and even success. The more you move forward, the more you learn and grow.

Sure, you can see how others deal with situations and model them as best you can, but we all deal with our situations differently. I have found from my experience over the years that using humor has helped me take the bite out of a lot of things that ordinarily would have been more of a struggle than they really were.

I've tried to continuously work on my personal development game, although lack of consistency, procrastination, and perfectionism have been issues for me over the years. When I became certified in NLP (Neuro-Linguistic Programming), I picked up so many helpful strategies that have assisted me interpret situations differently and allowed me to make adjustments that I would have initially called struggles. I became more adept at adapting to what I considered life's struggles, enabling me to identify that most of the time, the real struggle was simply between my ears. But it's my sense of humor that I always rely on to be that first voice response. My stand-up comedy/improv background has proven invaluable.

From the D To the A...

This isn't about the New York City subway. When I was in college, I struggled with accounting and calculus, earning a "D" in both. They were like huge anchors bringing my entire grade point average down. I had put off taking a statistics class, as I figured I would struggle with it as well, but I needed to pass this class to graduate. To get through it, I had to adjust my mindset and approach it with a more positive attitude.

I worked on changing my study habits, which required me to rewire how my brain looked at the subject of statistics. I looked at the patterns of the problems and started doing a lot of formulas and equations, and after a while, it became easier to solve the problems. All this preparation helped, and if I didn't know something, I asked right away. At this point, I had a very high level of confidence and I really knew what I was doing. Well, it turned out that for the final exam I got an "A"!

In the end, it wasn't as difficult as I had made it out to be. The important lesson is that I had proven to myself that if I put my mind to it, worked hard, and applied myself, it can be done (for most things). It doesn't mean I'm going to be a chemical engineer anytime soon, but I accomplished my goal.

Everyone has their failures. How else do you learn what not to do the next time around? And everyone has their successes. Everyone navigates through their challenges differently, so we can all learn from one another. There's more than one way to overcome obstacles in order to reach your goals and see your vision through. This is what makes us all unique! Some take the slow lane and others ride in the express lane, even though the end goal is the same.

I think part of eliminating the struggle is getting clarity on what you want, whether it's work-related, or what you want in a relationship. Where do you see yourself in five, ten, twenty years from now? The sooner you know what you want, the more time you can devote to achieving it. If there's a career change, jump in and go full throttle ahead.

Grand Central Terminal

When I became a docent at Grand Central Terminal in 2013, I drew upon what I had learned in that old statistics class. (A docent is a fancy name for a tour guide who doesn't get paid.) The new challenge was that I had to become certified, going through what they said was equivalent to an MBA-level program. So, how was I going to get through this study? I had been out of school and hadn't studied for something on this level in over 20 years. I had to prepare something in NYC to talk about and they were going to record me. Once I started the interview, the woman interviewing me could see my natural enthusiasm. I noticed that she was using the same model camera that I had, so I began to use an NLP technique to build rapport: "We have the same camera, what a great camera!" I tried to make her smile and elicit any kind of positive response. (Building rapport is a very effective NLP strategy.)

In the end, I was selected for their program! Hooray! Now what?! I looked back and tried to use a similar approach to how I had passed my statistics class as best I could. It was a long time ago, but the same study habits applied. Here I used another NLP strategy known as modeling. Just like for my statistics class, I blocked everything out around me and focused like I was on this "special ops" mission. Rather simply, I just immersed myself into Grand Central Terminal. I lived and breathed it. Anything related to Grand Central, I was on top of it. The key was welcoming the challenge with enthusiasm. I talked about things that I learned in having conversations with others until it just became part of my subconscious, and there were a lot of things to go over. At times it felt very overwhelming. I often told myself to stay positive, have fun, and don't put so much pressure on yourself. I learned a lot more after my first couple of tours, and going through the docent education program was an incredible learning and growing experience. Becoming a docent has made a big difference in my life, as I realized that I have a passion for history, and by adding a little humor in the mix, I can really bring my tours to life and found that people are much more engaged. The positive feedback I've received confirms this. I'm glad I stuck with the program, as it has been a very fulfilling experience for me and has also opened so many other doors. I am now a professional tour guide in NYC. You never know where things can lead or what other opportunities may present themselves to you!

You Can Do That?

After college, I worked on Wall Street as a stockbroker for a short time, then moved over to the trading desk. After a while, I felt it just wasn't for me, but the level of experience I had received was invaluable. After about a year on the trading desk, the creative side of my brain was saying it was time to move on. At the time, I didn't know where my income would come from once I left. I was talking with one of the traders one day and he asked, "Why don't you look at temping?" I said, "What's that?" He explained that I could work for some time and then have the option to stay on or go somewhere else, and sometimes it can turn into a full-time position. I was young and didn't even know that such a thing existed, so this is an excellent example of the importance of being aware of your options. There's a saying that goes like this: "You know what you know, you know what you don't know, and you don't know what you don't know." There's always something new that you can learn; this is what makes life an adventure. So, through temping at various jobs, I was able to support myself while still having the flexibility to pursue other interests.

Where There's a Will, There's a Way

In my NLP training, it says that unresourceful people do not exist, only unresourceful states. This served as a good example as I was visiting friends in Florida whom I had met earlier in the year on a trip to one of the Caribbean Islands. I went by myself, and it turned into one of the best decisions I'd ever made, as it developed into new relationships and a new circle of friends. I had forced myself to get out of my social comfort zone, as many of my friends at home were getting married and having kids, so we couldn't hang out as much as we used to do. There was a special price on a club membership where my Florida friends belonged. Considering that I was still living in NYC, I needed to make a list of the pros and cons of joining their club. Is this even feasible? How often would I get down to Florida to make it worthwhile? Can I afford to do this? I figured it's the same travel time whether it was a two-to-three-hour drive to the Hamptons, or to the Jersey Shore for a summer share (which I wasn't really into), or flying south to Florida where I had a place to stay with no lodging expenses. I decided to do it, despite that it might be a stretch financially when adding up food, drinks, and miscellaneous expenses.

So, I thought about what I could do to make some more money to cover these extras. I made up some funny sayings and put them on t-shirts and sold them while I was visiting, and to my surprise, I was able to cover most of my food and drink costs. Then, after about a year, I created a website and started selling t-shirts and other things online; and this is how I first got involved in affiliate marketing. Affiliate marketing has helped me bring in an extra income for many years, and this would've never happened if I had not stepped out of my comfort zone and looked at ways to become more resourceful. Where there's a will, there's a way.

Now, there were plenty of times being an affiliate marketer that I've often felt like I've been struggling through it, dealing with one technical issue after another that would throw me off for what seemed like hours or days. I could feel the frustration building and just wanted to throw the computer out the window. One thing that helped me get through it was to take a break and go for a walk in the park. There's something very therapeutic about being in nature. It helps to clear the noise from your head, and oftentimes, I would come home and figure out exactly what I needed to do. I'm currently working on various projects online, and I know that if I stay consistent, good things will happen.

Working in a Cartoon

Have you ever worked for someone that when you wake up in the morning, you're hoping it's the weekend? Well, I had that very feeling many times during the workweek. I had a boss who wasn't the easiest person to work for. She had mood swings, was overly demanding, and would say some of the craziest things that sometimes didn't make any sense. Now before me, there was another guy in my position who, from what I can recall, had gone out to lunch and never returned to work. (I wonder why?) He just left and never came back. I mean, how bad does it have to be for someone to leave without telling anyone and not return?! And here I was, his replacement. What was I getting myself into here? You kind of get a taste of it above. I seemed to be in her direct line of fire every day. If others saw her approaching, they would run the other way. I remember always saying to colleagues in the office that it was like working in a cartoon. They agreed! I didn't know it at the time, but I was using an NLP technique called Timeline Therapy, where you can dissociate and float up above your timeline, whether it be past, present, or future, and observe yourself and your surroundings in the scene below. (This is often used in visualization strategies, which is a very valuable skill set.) It felt like we were all in this wacky cartoon where green means stop and red means go. It was hysterical, yet our reality at the time.

Now I understand that people's behavior can change under stress. Stress can turn the nicest of people into monsters, and you don't have to wait for a full moon for this to happen. Combine that with sales quotas, deadlines, quarterly reports, and pressure from top execs, and you have yourself a tough situation. Dealing with the nine-to-five in a hostile environment is not my idea of a good time; but after work, my boss was a different person - she was actually nice! Every day, I wondered who would be showing up. It was like a Dr. Jekyll or Mr. Hyde scenario. "This is all gold for a comedian," is what I would say to myself in order to keep my sanity as I was on the verge of leaving. I had other people in the office telling me to hang in there and that things would be changing for the better very shortly.

At the time, I was doing stand-up comedy, and I had put together a new ten-minute set at one of the comedy clubs. It was mostly about my office experience, and I had a lot of material; many of my co-workers showed up to watch my set. There were plenty of laughs, and people in the audience could definitely relate to it, as they had their own office politics to deal with. It was a fun night all around and, in a way, it was also my therapy session. It was worth me waiting it out because there were changes to our business unit and she ended up leaving. I had great rapport with the guys I worked directly with. There was more latitude and flexibility and a very congenial working atmosphere with much less tension overall. This was one case where waiting it out paid off. So, don't underestimate the power of rapport. And having a sense of humor really helped, too.

Another time where my sense of humor helped me was at a temp job. (This was after three months, and from what I understand, there were around four other people before me in this position. They had trouble keeping anyone.) I had just gotten back from jury duty and received a call from HR asking me to please come up to see them. So, I sat down in their office and the woman in HR told me that it's not working out. I said to myself, "It may not be working out for you, but it's working out for me!" I never got a clear explanation as to why they let me go, as no one ever mentioned anything to me before this. As I left the building, walking down to the sidewalk, all I could think about was all the rain and flooding happening in the Midwest at the time. On the news, they showed the water levels up to the street signs. I thought to myself, "At least I don't have to swim home!" Imagine losing your job, and now you have to swim home! And just by saying that, it made me smile. It helped deal with that for the moment.

I found that using humor can act as a coping mechanism. I know we don't want to cope through life permanently. It's a protective coating that acts like a shield. It's good at deflecting all the crap being thrown your way. And this will give you time to address your issues and find solutions.

And don't be afraid to ask for help. Sometimes just by talking something through with someone can be very helpful. They can possibly help you come up with a game plan. I know who I can call to help me, and I know I can help others. Just work through the struggle and in the end, you usually find a way to work it out and see progress.

Iceland - A Meaningful Event

One of the things I learned in studying personal development over the years is that events in and of themselves have no meaning. We give meaning to events. Events are going on all around us, yet we don't attend or observe them because they may not have any meaning to us. So, don't create an issue where there isn't one.

This lesson reminds me of my trip to Iceland in 2006. This was the first time I had gone on a group trip where I didn't know anyone. Of course, the drama of certain events between a few people was inevitable, but I didn't let any of it bother me. These events had no meaning to me. I rose above the tide and stayed true to my mission, which was to experience Iceland. I was so focused on being in the moment; it was special. When you're standing on top of the continental tectonic plates that had collided into each other hundreds of thousands of years earlier and buckled up above ground, somehow the other "drama" around you pales in comparison. I had the most amazing time; and even though I didn't know anyone at the beginning, I still keep in touch with some of the people from that trip.

Another thing I took away from this adventure was that I didn't let friends who couldn't go because of conflicting schedules stop me from going. Some people never go anywhere because they don't have anyone to go with. Leaving your comfort zone is the only way to expand your horizons, and who knows, you may make new friends along the way.

Just a Little Extra

There were times when work wasn't consistent, causing a struggle to cover rent for a month here and there. I swore I would never be in this situation again, so I started to put a little extra away every month to build up a separate rent account. When my girlfriend moved in with me, she agreed to do the same, and each month, we would contribute more than what was necessary. Over time, it added up. If something should happen where someone loses their income, we had a safety cushion that gave us both some serious financial peace of mind. I'm grateful that we have this rent account, and it feels much better than the alternative. It's a tough road living paycheck to paycheck so just become a little more resourceful and you'll be surprised how much of a difference this can make. You may have to sacrifice some things in the beginning, but hopefully, you're able to see the future benefits.

Keep Scraping

I often go exploring around New York City, and once I visited the Tenement Museum on the Lower East Side of New York. This building has no plumbing and they have a replica of the outhouses outside. On this day, I had signed up for a tour through some of the apartments that were in the same physical condition as when they had unboarded them years earlier where 7,000 immigrants lived from 1863-1935. You can see all the layers of old paint on the walls, which reminded me of all the emotional baggage one would carry around that builds up over time, one layer on top of another. Most of us place a band-aid over our issues, and instead of scraping all the layers of paint off first and adding a new coat, we just paint over the old. The issues never really go away. They are still there, buried under more crap with the inner voice haunting you from time to time. What if we were able to scrape off all the layers first then start fresh? It is possible.

There are a couple of NLP techniques that have helped me with my negative internal dialogue. One of them is to change the tone of your inner voice. Replace your voice with a Mickey Mouse voice, for example, or some other character that helps take the seriousness away when you find yourself starting to beat yourself up verbally.

The other technique is the Meta Model strategy. So, I might say, for example: "I can't do anything right." The Meta Model would ask questions such as, "You can't do anything right, EVER?" There's not one thing that you've ever done, right? Did you get out of bed? Yes. Did you get dressed? Yes. Made yourself breakfast? Yes. Did you get to school or work? Yes." This is proof that the phrase "I can't do anything right" is a false narrative, and this sort of negative self-talk can get stuck in your subconscious mind, causing you to start playing the tape over and over. The dangerous part is that you really start to believe that you can't do anything when, in fact, it's not true. I've found the Meta Model a very effective tool at stopping those negative thoughts from permeating inside my head.

You can also learn how to look at things differently through reframing, which is another NLP technique where you can give a different meaning or context to a situation; therefore, the meaning of the situation changes. For example, you might see something one way, and then you're shown other possibilities and all of a sudden, the light bulb goes off and it is a wonderful moment when you know you have options and you're not stuck like you initially thought. It's something that you would not have been aware of otherwise, and there's a sense of relief and hope knowing that as you take action to help yourself move forward, you can persevere through the fog and become unstuck. Studying NLP has helped me to better understand the human condition and stuck states of behavior.

Changing your environment can also do wonders for finding solutions. What happens - at least in my experience - is that my negative inner voice starts to crash over me like a tidal wave. You need to implement a pattern-interrupt as fast as possible. Start repeating positive affirmations, as this will help tone down the negativity. Or, for example, I might turn on the radio and listen to a song from the '80s! All you need is a one-hit-wonder to do the trick! Playing a favorite song that makes you feel good will help change your state quickly. Start laughing at something, even at your own situation. It will help get your creative juices flowing, and a possible solution could be right around the corner. The worst thing is to do nothing to counter negative thoughts. You can make yourself sick from concentrating on negative thoughts. So, I found that staying positive, especially while struggling through whatever may be happening in life, is 100% better for my mental health. When you hear the phrase "stay positive," this is like your superpower. Positive thoughts can counter negative thoughts, and when you're negative, it's easy to become jaded and take on a victim mentality. I look at the power of positive thoughts as a gift that I can call upon while struggling through something.

Much Ado About Nothing

I remember when I first started doing stand-up comedy, I would get such anxiety getting ready to do a five-minute set. True story. I would get all worked up, and for what? I realized that it's only five minutes, and it goes quite fast when you're on stage. You blink and it's over. It seems like two deep breaths later and I'm done. I think much of life is like these five minutes. You get crazy and all worked up about something - drama, drama, drama - and in the end, it's much ado about nothing. Just know that it gets easier the more you do something. It did for me, and it will work for you. We must understand that no one ever got really good at anything by doing it just once so there's no point in beating yourself up over it. Instead, use it as a learning experience. This mindset has helped me when creating new tours as well. Just be as prepared as possible, have confidence in yourself, and have fun. You're the teacher/master, and they're the students. I've found that I can apply this principle to many areas of my life.

There are two sides to every situation, one positive and one negative; which one you decide to focus on will determine how much pleasure or pain you attract into your life. When it comes to my approach towards life, I live by a very common saying: "Always look on the bright side of life." I would often hear my grandmother say that the alternative is not an option. She was a very positive woman and was right. Look at it this way, if it's too bright, you can always put on sunglasses.

"Struggles are a part of life but they are not the totality of what life entails. So we must remember to discover all the other ingredients that make life worth living."

~ Unknown

CHAPTER ELEVEN

SURFING THE WAVES OF STRUGGLE

by Joy Chien

First Wave

My depression started four days before my birthday in Washington, DC on December 20th, 2012. It was a dark, snowy evening, and I was supposed to meet some friends for dinner. I was feeling pressured, stressed, and pushed by my co-founder, but mostly by my new boyfriend who wanted me to fly to Sweden for Christmas. I think I jumped into that relationship way too quickly. My startup business wasn't going as expected, and my co-founder and I weren't seeing eye to eye. I remember driving in the snow just out of my street, and then witnessing the headlight halo of the oncoming car and somehow gravitating towards it. I remember a soft voice pushing me to crash into that other car, whispering, "You need to do this." Why would I say this to myself? Some unconscious part of me wanted a wake-up call. The way I was living my life was not working for me anymore, and I felt terrified to make the changes I knew I needed to make. When I hit the oncoming car, it was a devastating crash. The driver of the other vehicle immediately emerged and started yelling at me, "What the

F is wrong with you?! You stupid f@#$ing bitch, you saw me, and you swerved right into me!" But at that moment, I had a tornado of emotions going on inside, and I just replied, "Here's my car insurance information, and please stop yelling at me. I'll pay for this, I promise." Thank goodness I was able to partially drive and push the car back home, ashamed and embarrassed — the mutilated car mirrored how I felt inside. A complete wreck. I didn't leave my house for the following few months.

Scary changes started months earlier when I decided to quit my comfortable, six-figure executive job at IBM right before the London summer Olympics. It was a really long and difficult decision. I had been practicing yoga and meditation for a few years; it helped me slow down enough to listen to my intuition. I felt shifts inside myself, and over time, I couldn't help but feel stuck doing something I wasn't passionate about. I felt that my colleagues valued routine, stability, and feeling safe in their comfort zone. Despite their unhappiness, they would never give up the comforts of a well-paid job or the certainty and security that came with it. I can't blame them. I was paralyzed with fear of making any career mistakes for over a decade. It's safe, and it's what everyone else did. But a certain part of me could not do it anymore; I craved adventure and did not want to spend the rest of my life buried under Excel and system requirements with only two weeks of vacation a year. I will never forget my glorious last day at work when I flew out the next day to attend the Olympics. It was so exciting! Pure, unbridled freedom. I felt like I had waited for this moment my entire life...finally free to create the life I wanted. I planned to travel and then start my own company with my best friend. I went traveling around Europe and Southeast Asia for six months on these long bus rides through Laos, Cambodia, Vietnam, and Myanmar, where I started to notice a lot of emotions and memories surfacing.

I just brushed it off and tried to ignore the negative thoughts. When I got back home, I had so much free time on my hands, I started to spiral into very harsh self-talk and self-doubt. First came the sleepless nights. All of a sudden, 4am became my prime time for the "what am I doing with my life" panic attacks, and journaling was the only thing that helped. These echoes of past voices just kept talking. In the deepest moments of my despair, I stopped feeling altogether. I was indifferent and detached in every aspect of life, which was a complete departure from my typically stubborn and opinionated self. Everyone kept saying, "You're starting your own company…I wish I could have your life," and in my head, it felt like World War III was going on. It was a really gruesome slaughter and dissolving of my former self-image. The craziest part was that I wasn't conscious of any of it. Life before this included planning every hour of the day, where I had no free time to be alone with my thoughts. This is where I felt safe, and as long as I kept moving, I couldn't get hurt — at least, that's what I thought.

Within a few months, I had torn down my entire sense of self and ripped apart all of the confidence that took me 30 years to build. I was so harsh, critical, and judgmental of myself. It's not like you wake up and say, "This is the day I'll ruin my life," but over time, that's exactly what happened. I couldn't seem to find any positive voices in my head, but I was drowning in a sea of self-doubt. For months after the accident, I would look in the mirror and cry in judgment for so long that my face would become red, swollen, and almost unrecognizable. I spent so many endless nights battling insomnia, paranoia, suicidal thoughts, and panic attacks; my brokenness resulted in extreme depression, afraid to even leave my house. Not knowing what to do, I began to obsessively research yoga teacher training programs, thinking that yoga might be the answer to set back on the road to feeling whole and complete. Of course, it couldn't and didn't. I completed a yoga teacher training in Bali. What I enjoyed the most was the yogic philosophy, but even that was not the fast fix I had dreamed of. The echoes of the past were still there.

The Second Wave

When I moved to Singapore in 2014, I didn't know anyone, and wanted to build up my social circles. I thought it would be easy to join the biggest social sports league called Dragonboating. It was beautiful; I met so many people and made new friends whom I trusted, or so I thought. To conclude a great first year in Singapore, I went to a Christmas celebration with my Dragonboat team. There was a lot of drinking and aggressive alpha male behavior, but I thought I was just being overly sensitive. The captain of the team tried to put his hand on my leg that evening to which I politely moved his hand and moved away. After the party, I went to change clothes, and the next thing I realized is that he was in the women's changing room. I was shocked; I froze. He used his physical strength to overpower me, there was nothing I could do. He violated me and then ran out. I told one of my teammates afterward what had happened while sharing a cab home. He asked, "Are you sure?" To which I replied, "Of course, I'm sure it just happened." He went silent.

I beat myself up a lot afterward because I thought that maybe it was my fault, or I could have done more to escape from the women's changing room. At the time, I knew he was a lot stronger than me, and I also knew that I could get seriously hurt if I tried to fight back. I confronted him the next day because I was so upset and wanted to think maybe it was just a big misunderstanding. I so desperately wanted to believe that. We met up at a bar, and he was nervously smoking and drinking. We talked for a while. Finally, I asked him, "Did you not hear me say, 'What are you doing? This is not ok...stop!'"

I didn't get an apology. He didn't even acknowledge my hurt feelings or ask me how I felt or if I was ok. He trivialized everything and talked about how his last girlfriend cheated on him. I felt so angry, disappointed, and humiliated; I just wanted to get out of there.

I wasn't planning to go to the police because I thought I could just forget about this and move on with my life. Like a bad dream, I could only suppress it like other negative emotions before. However, I would be sitting on the bus and then have a flashback, and all of a sudden feel so small, and then just burst into uncontrollable sobs. The same thing happened during meetings at work; I couldn't get the images out of my head that would trigger this feeling of helplessness, making me burst into tears. I had frequent panic attacks that would get so bad that I couldn't breathe. I didn't feel safe anywhere. It was like this base of safety that I stood on every day was just pulled out from under me. My boss ended my contract for underperforming. He even tried talking to me, asking, "What's happened the past couple months? The client says you keep leaving meetings abruptly and you're just not focused. Is it your boyfriend? I'm sorry, I have to let you go." I was devastated, and wanted support from my boyfriend, who was living in Sweden at the time. He told me not to go to the police and forget this ever happened to avoid getting retraumatized. He meant well, but I felt so abandoned and overwhelmed. We soon broke up. There was something very wrong; my body was having a far more significant reaction to the assault than my mind could rationalize.

I ended up going to the police after a month of being trapped in an inner tornado. The Singaporean uncle at reception nearly fell out of his seat when I told him I wanted to report a rape. I waited at the police station for seven hours, just to be denied. It was shocking how the officer said I waited too long, asked what I was wearing, and said he could call this guy and give him a warning as a favor to me. I had to call a friend who worked at the police station to intervene just to file the police report. I didn't want to leave until I was certain they filed a report against my attacker. Soon after, I was kicked off the Dragonboat team and told that I'm not welcome anymore. I was like a stain on the team that needed to be removed. Apparently, specific competitions were coming up, and it was easier to get rid of the newbie than the captain of the team. I went through many interviews with the police, and they asked me if I had a witness or if I had spoken to anyone right after the assault. I gladly gave the name of my teammate, whom I told right after; however, I didn't realize that he would lie under oath. I confronted him with hot, angry tears pouring from my eyes when I found out he didn't tell the truth and asked him, "Why didn't you tell the police what happened? I know you remember what I told you that night." He responded, "He (my attacker) already had called me, telling me to keep my mouth shut…we are friends, what could I do? He could be canned or imprisoned for life." The investigation went on for a year but got dismissed due to lack of evidence. I felt so crushed and abandoned by everyone. This incident had cost me my job, my ten-year-long relationship, my team, my friends, my dignity, and most of all, my feeling of safety in the world. I felt so sad that I couldn't even talk to my parents about what happened.

The Third Wave

When my boyfriend and I broke up, I also lost my best friend of ten years. I had never let my emotional guard down before, and in my depression, he was my only light — his bright beacon of hope gave me the strength and the positive voices I needed to get up again. That's probably why I couldn't deal with the sexual assault, because I was so dependent on him through my first depression. He was like a pillar in my emotional well-being. Having him in my life was like the sky was blue. I completely took him for granted. He was like my Band-Aid on the outside of a cracked bathtub full of a lifetime of emotions that I had not dealt with healthily.

At the beginning of the relationship, we could talk for hours about anything, and he felt so safe because we had been friends for years already. I loved the fact that he spoke multiple languages fluently (including Chinese); he was so sporty and smart. I moved to Sweden for a while and we traveled around Europe, Asia, and the US together. One night, while sailing through the Komodo islands, we were lying on the top deck of the boat staring at the stars. He asked what love felt like for me. I had to think about it for a while because I wanted to give an honest answer. I replied, "Fear, abandonment, and pain." I will never forget the look on his face. He was pretty shocked and had to process my answer. I asked him how love felt for him. He responded, "Like trust, acceptance, and safety." I was wondering what was wrong with this naive guy, and how did he ever get so brainwashed by Disney? I later reflected on if there was something wrong with me and why I started to feel so trapped and anxious in the relationship as time went on. I guess I expected imminent doom and planned for it. I had already written the ending for our relationship, and perhaps every relationship I have ever had.

When we broke up, I had no idea how to deal with all the negative voices I had suppressed, and again, spiraled into sleepless nights, panic attacks, and anxiety.

Rising from Depression

During my first depression, I was far too ashamed and embarrassed to share how I felt with anyone, including my parents. My boyfriend was the only one I could talk to. He was in Sweden at the time, but we would Facetime almost every day. He encouraged me to leave the house by simply walking to the mailbox. Later, he encouraged me to go on a retreat. It took months, but with his support, I worked up the courage to go for a surf camp. The surf camp is in a beautiful lush jungle in Costa Rica. The golden sunsets through the last palm trees and the night sky lit up with hundreds of fireflies which were so breathtaking. I had a difficult time there, though. Everyone else seemed so happy and carefree. It just made me very self-conscious of how stiff and anxious I was. Trying to surf was even more challenging and terrifying than I ever expected. I can still hear my instructor saying, "Let go of your board and pop up! Let it go in life and just go with the flow." I really couldn't let go then of who I thought I should be and what I should be doing.

Traveling and setting up little challenges for myself did help me gain confidence, little by little. In the beginning, it was just walking to the mailbox, then going to surf camp alone, and then solo traveling around Europe. I was finally living in the present moment again and not stuck regretting the past or worrying about how I had ruined my future. I had heard about this transformational ten-day meditation program from a friend and bought a ticket to the birthplace of Vipassana - Yangon, Myanmar. Unfortunately, I was expelled from the program for having food poisoning from something I ate my first day in Yangon. Since I was already in Myanmar, I decided to volunteer at a children's orphanage in Pha'an. It was one of the best things I've ever done. Talk about a lesson in gratitude! These impoverished little angels of love with no shoes were dirty and smelly but were so happy. I didn't have to do anything, and all of a sudden, just being with them - I was enough. I was accepted in their community. I watched people in the region celebrate life, appreciate life, and my problems paled in comparison. I began to wonder how I ever became so ungrateful and developed a sense of entitlement for happiness, for my health, for loving supportive friends and parents who would always be there for me.

I also met some very kind and compassionate ladies along the way. I tried to speak to myself the way they talked to me or their kids. Growing up, my parents never asked how I felt or comforted my feelings in a gentle, soft way. I adopted my friends' voices in my head. In particular, my friend Shirley would call me and ask, "How are you feeling, honey? What's wrong?" The way she said it and the tone of her voice was so warm and caring. I realized I had never talked to myself that way. Slowly, over time, instead of accusing, judging, criticizing, blaming, and shaming myself, I developed a kinder inner narrative.

Unraveling my Unconscious Fears

Like many multi-cultural children, I grew up quite nomadically, and lived on three continents before puberty. I was born in China, moved to England at age seven, and then to the US for high school and spent the next 18 years there. As a kid, I loved science and conducting experiments. Now, as an adult, I love setting up experiments around thoughts that are no longer serving me. I learned to trace my feelings of inadequacy, shame, helplessness, and abandonment to the first time I felt them. Feeling the trauma triggered lots of childhood memories.

I had a pretty great childhood, but I remember some sad moments where I was utterly helpless. My mom was quite busy as a university professor, doing a part-time MBA, and taking care of her adoptive mother who was dying of cancer. This meant I grew up without full-time parents until we moved to London, and my grandparents' parents were not especially fond of me since I was a girl. In traditional China, many girls were even killed because parents wanted boys to carry on the family name. My dad left for England when I was three. I didn't see him for four years. The feeling of helplessness and abandonment always goes back to this image of my parents leaving. I would desperately panic because I didn't know if I would ever see them again. My mom likes to joke that when I was two, I would sit in my crib grasping my soiled blanket soaked in urine and I wouldn't say anything because I was so scared. I remember how much my parents blew up whenever I did anything wrong as a child, spilled things, broke a glass, it felt like endless screaming about how careless and stupid I was. If I cried, I would get hit and yelled at until I stopped crying. To this day, I have never seen my parents cry, so this emotional constipation was just normal.

Over the years, incompetence became my inner dialogue until I was so paralyzed with fear of making mistakes, I couldn't do anything or make any decisions. I was tall and stupid. That's what my mom called me, and that's what I believed. It sounds abusive, but this is actually Chinese culture dating back for generations. You're not allowed to compliment or praise your children; otherwise, you would superstitiously ruin their life. With this in mind, China in the '80s was a very different place, and I don't think they were conscious of the impact of their words or actions. They wanted the best for me and migrated to new continents just so I could have a better life.

Now, instead of telling my inner child how pathetic and what a loser she is for constantly feeling terrified and sad, I took the parts of myself that I felt ashamed of and invited them back into my life. I accepted them. No longer suppressing my inner child or the negative emotions, I started to have a dialog with her. The first time I spoke to my inner child was in this journal entry:

September 6th, 2014

I'm journaling in the moonlight, living the dream of my 20s, listening to the waves crashing, enjoying the fresh, crisp smell of the ocean listening to Etta James - At Last.

Man, I'm really loving being by myself right now. I have so much clarity. This is so calming, the scenery of the silvery waves dancing on the ocean is just breathtaking. I love being with myself. Well at least on Ko Samui haha.

I love you. I will never leave you again. I'm sorry I judge to you, abandoned you, ignored and dismissed you for so long. I didn't listen to you and locked you up because you scared me. I became so afraid of being alone. Being with you. I only cared about what others thought of me. I felt safe and loved in someone else's arms and never on my own. I thought as long as I kept moving, I would never have to face you. But you followed me. Well, I am ready and you can come out now. I want to hear everything. I'm here for you. I am going to make an amazing home for you.

A real place you can call home, with people who support you and who care about you. A place where you feel safe and excited to be! A place that makes your heart sing. We're going to commit to each other and eventually to someone who brings out the best in us. Someone who gives us butterflies, makes us feel loved, at home and cares about. We are going to create a life that we want, on our own terms. I want to wake up every morning, not because of some alarm, but because we cannot wait to live the life we choose, we created, where we are finally free to thrive, live and experience. Let's commit to having way more fun.

The truth is you are good enough, smart enough, strong enough, pretty enough. When we fall, I promise to listen and grieve for the losses, the pain, and sadness. Then we will get right back up! No matter what, we will always have each other from our first breath to our last.

XO,

Your always bestie

Reflections

Depression is not about feeling unhappy, because when I'm unhappy, at least I'm still feeling something. Instead of seeing the world in vibrant colors, I could only see it in black and white. Life was dull and cloudy. I couldn't snap out of it. What made it worse is when others told me to snap out of it. I felt like I was living in a shell of my former self — like I was dying inside, and I felt completely helpless. I was chasing happiness and seeking solutions from everyone except the one person who could actually make a change — me.

Looking back now, seven years after my first wave of depression, I can honestly say that the last year and a half has been great. I have a fantastic home, living with a beautiful best friend and mentor. I slowly built my sense of self back by doing little things to help other people. I would get feelings of calm contentment or praise from my awesome friends, or acknowledgment from a consulting gig, or feedback from people at a Me Too rally. Every talk I gave at the Singapore Sports Council or the Singapore police, I felt myself getting a little bit stronger. I had something to offer the world again, and with a consistent practice of gratitude, I was so grateful for good days again.

I've been a private investor, which was my only means of making money during this long period of transition and personal development, and now I'm teaching others how to invest in the stock market. I've been invited to give talks on entrepreneurship and women's empowerment. I recently got back from a local women's financial literacy workshop and conference in the Maldives, which was so rewarding.

During my first wave of depression, I was still hosting startup competitions and remember running a startup weekend in DC. This guy came to talk to me afterward and said, "It's so cool that you started your own company, an award-winning coworking group, and it just seems like you have this picture-perfect life. Well done for having it together." I remember feeling like such an imposter, not owning my success or allowing myself to receive love or praise. After that weekend, I confided in this kind stranger about how bad it was inside. I will never forget his words: "I know how you feel. After every winter, no matter how dark or how cold it can get, there is always the spring.

Some days I wonder why it took me so many years to recover from depression. I believe resilience is like a muscle. You can train it. You can get up faster each time. You can develop the best relationship of your life with yourself first. Everything else will fall into place after.

Thank you to my darkest days for the appreciation and gratitude I now have for my greatest days.

> **"If there is no struggle, there is no progress."**
>
> ~ Frederick Douglass

Author Biographies

John Spender

Chapter One

John Spender is a 17-time International Best Selling co-author, who didn't learn how to read and write at a basic level until he was ten years old. He has since traveled the world started many businesses leading him to create the best-selling book series *A Journey Of Riches*; he is an Award Winning International Speaker and Movie Maker.

John was an international NLP trainer and has coached thousands of people from various backgrounds through all sorts of challenges. From the borderline homeless to very wealthy individuals, he has helped many people to get in touch with their truth to create a life on their terms.

John's search for answers to living a fulfilling life has taken him to work with Native American Indians in the Hills of San Diego, the forests of Madagascar, swimming with humpback whales in Tonga, exploring the Okavango Delta of Botswana and the Great Wall of China. He's traveled from Chile to Slovakia, Hungary to the Solomon Islands, the mountains of Italy and the streets of Mexico.

Everywhere his journey has taken him; John has discovered a hunger among people to find a new way to live, with a yearning for freedom of expression. His belief that everyone has a book in them was born.

He is now a writing coach having worked with more than a 170 authors from 34 different countries and his publishing house MotionMediaInternational has published 20 non-fiction titles to date.

He also co-wrote and produced the movie documentary *Adversity* starring Jack Canfield, Rev. Micheal Bernard Beckwith, Dr. John Demartini and many more, coming soon in 2020. Moreover, you can bet there will be the best-selling book to follow!

Georgiana Zor

Chapter Two

After graduating from high school in Romania, she studied European Studies and obtained a Master's degree in Crisis & Security Management from Leiden University's in The Netherlands.

Although not published before, Georgiana has always loved writing. Composing poems from an early age, writing pieces for school magazines, creating short stories, and journaling since she was nine.

Georgiana loves of being in nature, especially close to the sea and the starry night sky. She likes exploring cities by getting lost through narrow streets and buildings that tell stories. She loves art in any form. Georgiana loves painting portraits birthed by her imagination.

She gets her energy from inspirational people who have interesting stories and an avid love for life. Georgiana is in love with British humor. She is trying to improve herself constantly – recently, she took acting lessons and is learning how to fly an airplane.

Brian Wood

Chapter Three

Brian Wood is obsessed with personal development, believing it is our responsibility to inspire others to take action and drive positive change. He is the past Chairman of the Board for the Tempe Chamber of Commerce, with his term concluding in July 2017. Originally, from NJ, Brian earned his BA in Communications from William Paterson University. He earned his MBA in 2014 from the University of Phoenix while balancing family, community involvement and corporate life. Brian has been an Executive Coach with the American Express Leadership Academy hosted by the Lodestar Center for Philanthropy and nonprofit innovation at Arizona State University - for the past three years.

Additionally Brian is: a Certified Professional Coach (leadership and transition); Founder of MARS Coaching - Myrtlewood Athlete Representation and Success; a Board

Member with "Linking Sports and Communities"; a Mentor with New Pathways for Youth; a Certified Agent with FIBA, the NBA and WNBA Players Associations; and a graduate of Valley Leadership – the legendary Class 32!

Brian was certified as a professional coach through the Institute for Professional Excellence in Coaching (IPEC), and uses a model that identifies the mindset and energy that is constructive while attacking the opportunities to convert catabolic thinking. Brian is enthusiastic about helping people and organizations find their passion, identifying and achieving their definition of success – while enjoying the journey and leveraging their "gifts." He loves adventure, travel and time with his wife Vivian and family. A writer and a speaker, Brian also enjoys reading and is grateful to watch his children compete athletically and in the game of life.

Erin Levee

Chapter Four

Erin began her meditation journey at the age of seventeen, learning transcendental meditation from Tim Brown. Her absolute immersion into silence was a turning point and led to many years of travelling through India and to the teachings of Ramana Maharishi.

Since then, sitting with esteemed Satsang teachers Gangagji, Mooji and Isaac Shapiro led to a grounding in her personal life and now married, with two young children, Erin feels drawn to offer her experience to those wishing to experience meditation for the first time. Trained in yoga therapy with Nikola Ellis at Adore yoga, and Aura soma colour therapy from the international school of ASIACT, she brings many healing modalities to her sessions and empowers others to choose wellness on all levels of their being.

She is a Doterra Silver leader and wellness advocate, empowering women in new ways of doing business collaboratively and with support from each other, their families and Mother Earth.

Www.spaciousbeing.com.au

M: 0415099705

Amy Suiter

CHAPTER FIVE

Amy Suiter is first and foremost a wife and a mother of three beautiful young souls, which in her world is the life of her dreams. She and her husband Dustin were high school sweethearts and have been together for 22 years and married for 12. They have three amazing children Haley (9), Trey (7), and Cash (2) they are the light in her world and definitely her why.

Amy played collegiate softball at the University of Washington and graduated with a Bachelor of Science in Psychology. After college, Amy started her collegiate softball coaching career at Texas Tech University where she pursued a doctorate program in Sports Psychology.

Western Washington University was the second and final stop in her twelve-year softball coaching career. Currently, Amy is taking her organizational leadership expertise, communication skills, and mindset coaching that she mastered in her playing and coaching career to athletes, organizations and businesses around the world.

Sonja Stamenova

CHAPTER SIX

Sonja Stamenova is born 29th August 1975 in a small town Sveti Nikole in the Republic of Macedonia. During her school years, she always showed interest in literature and even wrote poems that didn't have a chance to be published. In 1997 she moved to Australia to start a new life.

Sonja had two daughters and dedicated most of her time to her family but never gave up on her dream to become a writer and help people with her work. She is working in hospitality at the moment and is trying to endeavor her desire to become a writer.

Sonja enjoys reading, spending time with her family, cooking, traveling the world and doing charity work. In her life, she has been through a variety of tough times but never lost hope and now she tries to help other people by telling her stories and giving advice to others.

Andrea Daylor

Chapter Seven

A ndrea is from a large Italian, Irish family, born and raised in Pennsylvania. Andrea earned her degree in Occupational Therapy from Misericordia University in Dallas, Pa. She specialized in Hand and Upper Extremity Rehabilitation early in her career later entering corporate management.

Andrea resides in Jacksonville, Florida, with her family. She attributes her many blessings to God and the love and support of her parents, William and Michelina Daylor as well as her family, Michael and sons, Bryce, Rowan, and Anthony.

Anastasia Gunawan

Chapter Eight

As a young millennial, Anastasia is passionate about sharing her discovery to authentic success with others. An old paradigm of hard work equals success led Anastasia to a path of burn out and debilitating symptoms of chronic disease. She is a social epidemiologist, outdoor enthusiast, author, writer, health educator, and a yogi in training.

She is the founder of *The Burn Out Millennial* – a grassroots online movement with a simple mission to end stress and burn out epidemic https://theburnoutmillennial.com

She currently lives in Reno, NV with her loving partner and enjoys being an active member in her local community.

Lillian Tahuri

CHAPTER NINE

Lillian Tahuri has a background in central and local government working across strategy, policy, planning, compliance and the implementation of legislation. She is also a personal development, transformational and leadership coach. Lillian works with individuals and groups to create better leaders, on trauma, phobias, high performance and positive mindset tools to improve the lives of her clients.

She is passionate about the environment, human rights, gender equality, diversity and inclusion. She is currently a board member of UN Women Aotearoa New Zealand National and represents the board on the Women's Empowerment Principles Committee (WEPs).

Lillian is from New Zealand and has successfully represented her tribe to settle historical claims against their government. She holds a Bachelor of Arts (Humanities) in Philosophy from Massey University in New Zealand, a Neuro Linguistic Programming (NLP) Master Coach, Master Hypnotist and trained in neuroscience-based personal development.

Jason Stein

Chapter Ten

Jason Stein is a humorist and communicator, with a passion for sharing new experiences with others so they can learn. He is a professional tour guide in New York City, uniting his love of history with his background in improv and standup comedy.

Jason also approaches learning through personal development. He is a certified Practitioner of Neuro-Linguistic Programming (NLP), Transformational Coaching and Leadership, and focuses his coaching efforts on ways people can create financial security for themselves and their families.

Jason enjoys hiking and spending time in nature to fuel his creativity, positive mindset and sense of humor. He is excited to join with all the talented writers in this book on resilience.

To contact Jason for more information, please visit: www.thehappinesshelper.com

Joy Chien

Chapter Eleven

While at the FBI, Joy quit her corporate job seven years ago and transitioned to being a full-time private investor and has since been traveling the world, founded two companies; living her best life on her own terms.

Joy studied Bio Engineering and IT, founded an award winning co-working group The DC Nightowls, volunteers for Singapore's oldest women's rights NGO AWARE, hosts startup competitions and runs investing and yoga retreats around the world.

She's worked with individual investors as well as MNC's such as IBM, Accenture, Bloomberg, KPMG, Paypal, Hilton, etc.

With 15+ years of consulting and 12 years of stock market experience, Joy believes in a balanced, holistic approach to life especially when investing money.

As a financial wellness coach, she is now empowering other women to be financially independent and is working on an App to make researching stocks more fun and engaging. Joy is currently living in Singapore.

"Strength doesn't come from winning. Your struggles develop your strengths. When you go through hardships and decide not to surrender, that is strength."

~ Arnold Schwarzenegger

Afterword

I hope you enjoyed the collection of heartfelt stories, wisdom and vulnerability shared. Storytelling is the oldest form of communication, and I hope you feel inspired to take a step toward living a fulfilling life. Feel free to contact any of the authors in this book or the other books in this series.

The proceeds of this book will go to the Bali Street Kids Project, in Denpasar, Bali.

The project gives orphaned and abandoned children a home, meals and an education.

You can donate to this fantastic cause here: https://ykpa.org/

Other books in the series are…

In Search of Happiness : A Journey of Riches, Book Seventeen

https://www.amazon.com/dp/B07R8HMP3K

Tapping into Courage : A Journey of Riches, Book Sixteen

https://www.amazon.com/dp/B07NDCY1KY

The Power Healing : A Journey of Riches, Book Fifteen

https://www.amazon.com/dp/B07LGRJQ2S

The Way of the Entrepreneur: A Journey Of Riches, Book Fourteen

https://www.amazon.com/dp/B07KNHYR8V

Discovering Love and Gratitude: A Journey Of Riches, Book Thirteen https://www.amazon.com/dp/B07H23Q6D1

Transformational Change: A Journey Of Riches, Book Twelve

https://www.amazon.com/dp/B07FYHMQRS

Finding Inspiration: A Journey Of Riches, Book Eleven

https://www.amazon.com/dp/B07F1LS1ZW

Building your Life from Rock Bottom: A Journey Of Riches, Book Ten

https://www.amazon.com/dp/B07CZK155Z

Transformation Calling: A Journey Of Riches, Book Nine

https://www.amazon.com/dp/B07BWQY9FB

Letting Go and Embracing the New: A Journey Of Riches, Book Eight

https://www.amazon.com/dp/B079ZKT2C2

Making Empowering Choices: A Journey Of Riches, Book Seven

https://www.amazon.com/Making-Empowering-Choices-Journey-Riches-ebook/dp/B078JXMK5V

The Benefit of Challenge: A Journey Of Riches, Book Six

https://www.amazon.com/dp/B0778S2VBD

Personal Changes: A Journey Of Riches, Book Five

https://www.amazon.com/dp/B075WCQM4N

Dealing with Changes in Life: A Journey Of Riches, Book Four

https://www.amazon.com/dp/B0716RDKK7

Making Changes: A Journey Of Riches, Book Three

https://www.amazon.com/dp/B01MYWNI5A

The Gift In Challenge: A Journey Of Riches, Book Two

https://www.amazon.com/dp/B01GBEML4G

From Darkness into the Light: A Journey Of Riches, Book One

https://www.amazon.com/dp/B018QMPHJW

Thank you to all the authors that have shared aspects of their lives in the hope that it will inspire others to live a bigger version of themselves. I heard a great saying from Jim Rohan "You can't complain and feel grateful at the same time." at any given moment we have a chose to either feel like a victim of life or connected and grateful for it. I hope this book helps you to feel grateful and go after your dreams.

www.ingramcontent.com/pod-product-compliance
Lightning Source LLC
LaVergne TN
LVHW051553070426
835507LV00021B/2553